MYTHS and LEGENDS
ULTIMATE HANDBOOK

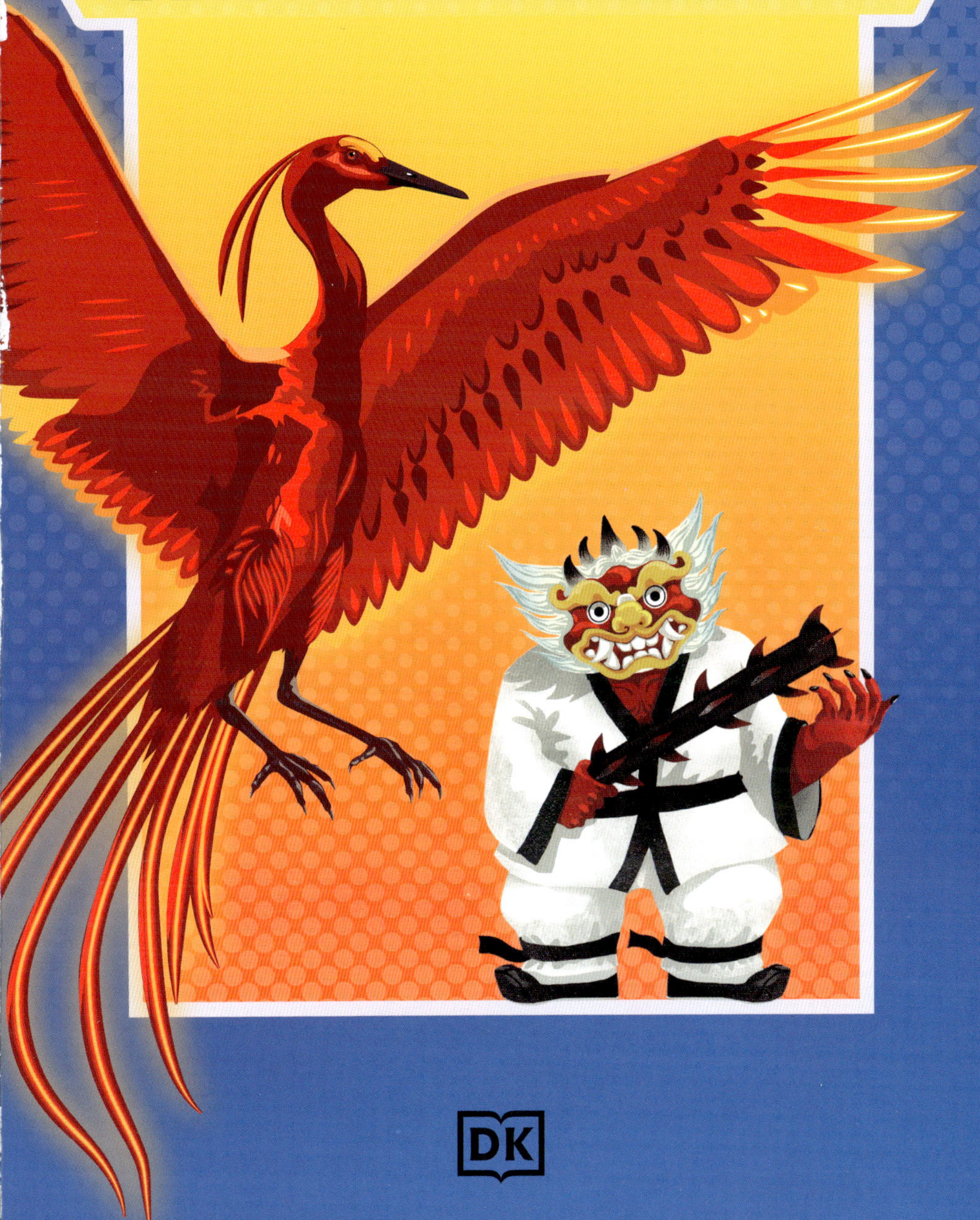

DK

DK | Penguin
Random
House

Senior Editor Kritika Gupta
Senior Art Editor Roohi Rais
Senior Jacket Designer Rashika Kachroo
Project Editor Abi Maxwell
Editor Syed Tuba Javed
Art Editor Nishtha Gupta
Senior Picture Researcher Sakshi Saluja
Picture Researcher Ridhima Sikka
Pre-Production Coordinator Vishal Bhatia
Pre-Production Designers Anita Yadav, Bimlesh Tiwari
Pre-Production Image Editor Vijay Kandwal
Jacket & Sales Material Coordinator Elin Woosnam
Managing Editor Roohi Sehgal
Managing Art Editors Diane Peyton Jones, Ivy Sengupta
Production Editor Becky Fallowfield
Senior Production Controller Ben Radley
Delhi Creative Head Malavika Talukder
Associate Publisher Gemma Farr
Art Director Mabel Chan

Illustrators Dan Crisp, Mohd Zishan
Consultants Jean Menzies, Leanne Holt,
Nozomi Tolworthy, Tim Topper

First published in Great Britain in 2025 by
Dorling Kindersley Limited
20 Vauxhall Bridge Road, London SW1V 2SA

The authorised representative in the EEA is
Dorling Kindersley Verlag GmbH. Arnulfstr. 124,
80636 Munich, Germany

A CIP catalogue record for this book is
available from the British Library.

ISBN: 978-0-2416-8670-6

Printed and bound in China

www.dk.com

MYTHS and LEGENDS
ULTIMATE HANDBOOK

Written by Ben Hubbard

Contents

GODS AND GODDESSES

HEROES, VILLAINS, AND MONSTERS

How this book works

Ready to read about awe-inspiring gods, goddesses, heroes, monsters, and mythical creatures? Here is some information to help you find your way around this book.

Profiles

The profiles sit within different chapters, each focusing on a different theme. These pages are packed with rich information, vivid illustrations, and descriptive annotations.

Super facts panels are filled with amazing details, including pronunciations and origins.

Want to find a particular profile? Look it up in the index on pp.282–287.

Not sure what a word means? Look it up in the glossary on pp.278–281.

Extra images highlight an interesting aspect about the character or creature.

Battle up!

These pages showcase exciting mythical battles between deities and monsters, as well as between heroes and villains.

Key information about the characters

Two powerful beings clash with each other across the page.

The winner is announced at the bottom of the page.

The stage for the battle is set in the introduction.

Special features

Feature pages provide extra information about mythologies from around the world. What are shapeshifters? How did Zeus become king of the Olympians? Read on to find out.

Striking picture with useful information to help explain

Stories through time

People have told stories since the beginning of human history. These stories helped our ancestors make sense of the world. They explained how the Sun rose and why rain fell. They gave meaning to nature, life, and the Universe.

Narasimha, the fourth avatar of the Hindu god Vishnu, had the head of a lion and the body of a human.

Religious stories

Most religions often have stories that explain their beliefs, rituals, and ideas about right and wrong. These religious stories usually involve humans, creatures, and gods interacting together. In some stories, gods like Vishnu come down to Earth in different forms to defeat evil kings or demons.

People who claim to have seen the Loch Ness Monster say it has flippers and a long neck.

Legends

Legends are typically stories about people and creatures that may have existed or events that may have happened in the past – even though they cannot be proved to be true. Some of the popular legendary creatures from around the world include the Loch Ness Monster and Bigfoot.

Folklore

The folklore of different cultures usually includes entertaining stories that are traditionally handed down by word of mouth from one generation to the next. They often include characters that educate about a culture's beliefs.

A gnome is a tiny, goblin-like creature or earth spirit from European folklore.

The ancient Greeks believed that Zeus threw thunderbolts to cause thunder and lightning.

Sacred stories

Some cultures tell stories featuring sacred creatures. Lizards are sacred to the New Zealand Māori, and some tribes believe that a spiritual reptile guards the house of Miru, the ruler of the underworld. The Māori mythological taniwha (*ta-nee-wah*) were supernatural beings that sometimes took the form of a giant lizard.

In Māori stories, the explorer Kupe was said to have a taniwha, a whale named Tuhirangi, that protected him.

Myths

Myths can be stories about how everything began and why certain things happen. They often feature creatures, heroes, and gods, such as the Greek god Zeus.

Ice and fire worlds

According to Norse mythology, the Universe began with the ice world, Niflheim [*NIF-el-hame*], and the fire world, Muspelheim [*MUS-pel-hame*]. Melting ice from Niflheim created Ymir [*EE-meer*], the frost giant. When he was later killed by Odin, Ymir's body formed the land and his blood created the water.

Ymir's huge skull was used to make the dome of the sky above the Earth.

Stories of creation

Every culture has a story about how the Universe began. Some myths say it was born from black nothingness or an endless ocean. Others think the world was hatched from a golden egg or formed from a giant's body. Often, creator gods and goddesses helped make the land and people.

The serpent's path

In West African folklore, the creator goddess Mawu made the world with the help of the male serpent Aido-Hwedo [*ah-ee-doh hweh-doh*]. By moving around in massive circles, they both shaped the Earth like a piece of round fruit. Aido-Hwedo then slithered across the land to carve out rivers, valleys, and mountains.

The eternal realm

In First Australian folklore, the creation period is called the "Jukurrpa", or "Dreamtime". During this time, ancestral beings in human and animal form moved across the desert - singing, marrying, fighting, and helping one another. This created the features of the land and its people, animals, and plants.

First Australian rock art depicting the Dreamtime spirit of a mother and child with a fish.

The golden egg

In Hindu mythology, the world began with an endless cosmic ocean. Floating in this ocean was a giant golden egg. Brahma, the creator god, hatched himself from this egg and its shell turned into the heavens above and the land below. Brahma, Vishnu, and Shiva then became the leading gods of the world.

Part of the Seneca creation myth depicted on a pottery dish

On the turtle's back

The Indigenous Seneca people believed that the Universe began with a sky and an ocean. One day, a woman fell from the sky into the ocean and sea creatures decided to save her. A toad collected mud from the seafloor and put it on a turtle's back to make land for the woman to live on.

Gods and goddesses

All-powerful gods and goddesses appear in the mythology of many cultures around the world. Most are supernatural beings with control over the world, nature, and people. Some gods and goddesses are kind and benevolent, while others are cunning, cruel, and self-centred.

The cosmic war

The Greek universe began with two supreme creators, Gaia (*GEY–a*) and Uranus (*YOOR–an–uss*). They made the world and gave birth to three groups of children – the one–eyed cyclops (*SAI–klops*), the hundred–handed giants, and 12 super–beings, called the Titans.

Also called Ouranos, Uranus was the primordial god of the sky.

Children of the primordial gods

Uranus was neither a good husband to Gaia nor a good father to the Titans. Gaia gave the Titan Kronos (*KHRO-noss*) a sharp sickle and told him to kill Uranus. Afterwards, Kronos married Rhea (*REE-a*), who gave birth to their children, later known as the Olympians.

Gaia was the primordial goddess of the Earth.

Leader of the Titans

Kronos became worried that his children would overthrow him, as he had done to Uranus. To prevent this, he ate his five children. When Rhea gave birth to their son Zeus, she tricked Kronos by giving him a stone wrapped in baby clothes instead of the baby. Kronos quickly devoured it.

The war between the Titans and Olympians was called Titanomachy.

Father versus son

Zeus grew up in secret on the Greek island of Crete. When he was an adult, he posed as a cupbearer for Kronos to give him a poisoned drink. As a result, Kronos vomited up the five children he had eaten. This started the great battle between Kronos's children (the Olympians) and the Titans.

Zeus shown on a throne as the king of Olympus

A painting depicting Mount Olympus

Olympians

With the help of the cyclops, the Olympians were victorious over the Titans. Zeus freed certain Titans and punished others, such as Atlas, whom he tasked with holding up the sky. Zeus and his five siblings then ruled from their palace on Mount Olympus.

Zeus

Super facts

Pronunciation: ZYOOSS
Meaning: The sky father
Origin: Greek mythology
Location: Greece and western coast of Türkiye (Turkey)   **Other names:** Jupiter, Jove   **Powers:** Control over weather and lightning, superstrength, shapeshifting
Symbols: Eagle, oak tree

King of the gods, wielder of the thunderbolt, and ruler of Mount Olympus, Zeus was the most powerful Greek deity. He controlled the weather and settled many divine disputes.

On Earth, I often shapeshift into an animal, like a cuckoo, bull, or swan. Back on Olympus, I'm the big man with a bushy beard.

Zeus wielded lightning-shaped thunderbolts, ready to be thrown at enemies.

As king of the gods, Zeus often sat on his throne in the heavenly realm of Mount Olympus.

Poseidon

God of the sea, water, and earthquakes, Poseidon was powerful, unpredictable, and vindictive. He rode a chariot pulled by seahorses and stirred up storms against ships that annoyed him.

> With my trident, I shatter rocks, shake the Earth, and bring about terrible winds and waves at sea.

Three-pronged trident

Super facts

Pronunciation: poh-SAI-don **Meaning:** Husband of the Earth **Origin:** Greek mythology **Location:** Greece and western coast of Türkiye (Turkey) **Other name:** Neptune
Powers: Control over the sea, tides, and earthquakes, superstrength, shapeshifting
Symbols: Trident, bull, horse, rock

Demeter

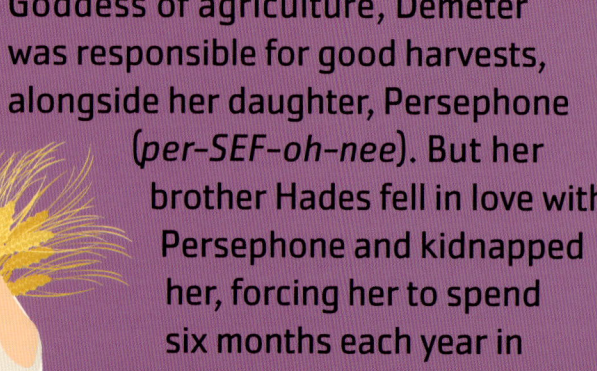

Goddess of agriculture, Demeter was responsible for good harvests, alongside her daughter, Persephone (*per–SEF–oh–nee*). But her brother Hades fell in love with Persephone and kidnapped her, forcing her to spend six months each year in the underworld.

Demeter was often shown with sheaves of wheat to symbolize her role in agriculture.

Every autumn and winter I mourn for my daughter, Persephone, which is why plants don't grow during that time.

Super facts

Pronunciation: deh-MEE-ter   **Meaning:** Earth mother
Origin: Greek mythology   **Location:** Greece and western coast of Türkiye (Turkey)   **Other names:** Sito, Thesmophoros
Powers: Control over harvest, fertility, and seasons
Symbols: Cornucopia, wheat, torch, bread

Hades

Hades was the god of the underworld, the land where the dead dwelled. Here, Hades judged deceased people and punished the wicked.

Hades was usually depicted with a crown as he was the ruler of the underworld.

Super facts

Pronunciation: HEY-deez
Meaning: The unseen one
Origin: Greek mythology
Location: Greece and western coast of Türkiye (Turkey) **Other names**: Clymenus, Eubouleus **Powers**: Ability to rule souls in the underworld, control of Earth's riches, invisibility **Symbols**: Narcissus (daffodil, cypress tree, pomegranate, chariot

I hardly ever venture above ground to see my siblings.

Aphrodite

Super facts

Pronunciation: aff-roh-DAI-tee
Meaning: Foam-born   **Origin:** Greek mythology   **Location:** Greece and western coast of Türkiye (Turkey)
Other names: Cytherea (Lady of Cythera), Cypris (Lady of Cyprus)
Powers: Control over love and desire, power over water
Symbols: Dove, pomegranate, swan, myrtle

The most beautiful Greek deity, Aphrodite was the goddess of love, fertility, and seafaring. Every god wanted to marry her, but Zeus made her marry the god Hephaestus (*heh–FEE-stuss*).

I was honoured as a goddess of war in Sparta, Thebes, and Cyprus.

According to legend, Aphrodite was born in the sea and brought to land on a shell.

Hera

The goddess of marriage and the sky, Hera was also the wife of Zeus. However, the couple quarrelled constantly, which caused trouble for the other gods, heroes, and humans.

Hera was usually shown carrying a long spear.

I was once so angry with Zeus that I sent serpents to kill his baby son, Heracles. However, Heracles strangled them!

Super facts

Pronunciation: HEER-a
Meaning: Lady
Origin: Greek mythology
Location: Greece and western coast of Türkiye (Turkey) **Other names**: Goddess of marriage, protector of women
Powers: Influence over marriages and childbirth, shapeshifting
Symbols: Peacock, pomegranate, lily, diadem

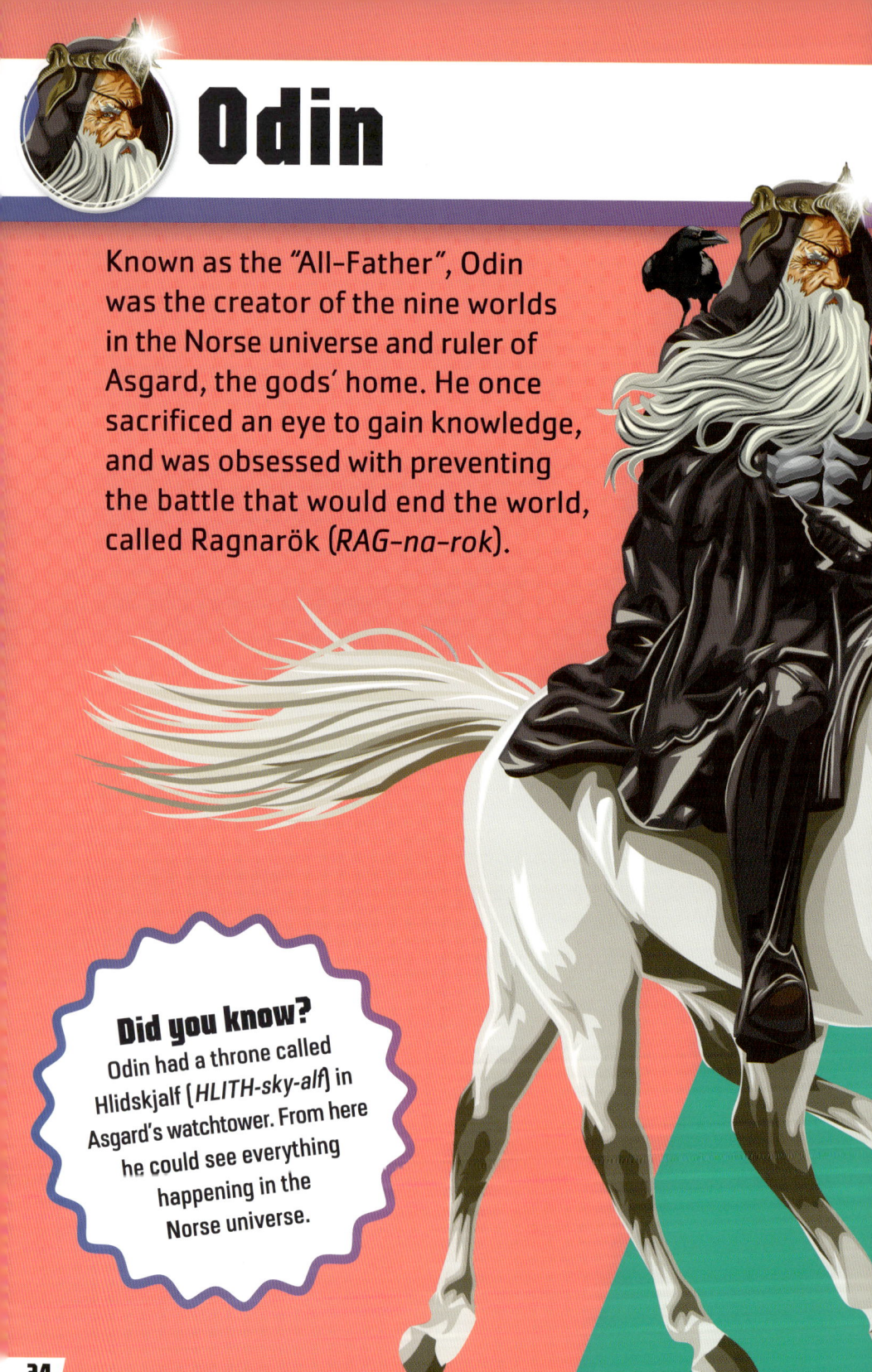

Odin

Known as the "All-Father", Odin was the creator of the nine worlds in the Norse universe and ruler of Asgard, the gods' home. He once sacrificed an eye to gain knowledge, and was obsessed with preventing the battle that would end the world, called Ragnarök (*RAG-na-rok*).

Did you know?

Odin had a throne called Hlidskjalf (*HLITH-sky-alf*) in Asgard's watchtower. From here he could see everything happening in the Norse universe.

Super facts

Pronunciation: OH-din **Meaning:** Supreme god
Origin: Norse mythology **Location:** North Atlantic and northern Europe
Other names: All-Father, Wodan (Woden or Wotan)
Powers: Incredible wisdom, ability to see into the future, shapeshifting, mastery over runes
Symbols: Pair of ravens, triple horn, Viking rune, wolf

Odin's spear, called Gungnir (*GUNG-neer*), was a special gift made by the Norse dwarfs.

Sleipnir (*sleyp-nir*) was a magical, eight-legged horse gifted to Odin by the trickster god, Loki.

Hugin (*HOO-ghin*) and Munin (*MOO-nin*) were Odin's ravens that sat on his shoulders and brought him news from across the Universe. In old Norse, Hugin means "thought" and Munin means "mind".

Thor

The fearless, red–bearded Norse god Thor loved to battle against the giants with his magical hammer, Mjölnir (*mee–YOL–neer*). He was the defender of Asgard and his mortal enemy was the evil Midgard Serpent, Jörmungandr (*YOR–mun–gan–der*).

> My hammer, Mjölnir, always sprang back to me after I threw it – no matter where or how far.

Was mostly shown wearing battle armour

Super facts

Pronunciation: th-orr   **Meaning:** Thunder
Origin: Norse mythology   **Location:** North Atlantic and northern Europe   **Other names:** Thunaer, Thunor
Powers: Ability to summon thunder and lightning, superstrength
Symbols: Hammer, compass, pair of ravens

Loki

The trickster Norse god Loki lived to cause mayhem and mischief. It was said that Loki, the son of a giant and a goddess, would fight against the gods at the battle of Ragnarök and bring about their doom.

Although Loki could shapeshift, he would usually appeared in human form.

Super facts

Pronunciation: LOW-kee
Meaning: Destroyer
Origin: Norse mythology
Location: North Atlantic and northern Europe
Other name: Lopt
Powers: Shapeshifting, ability to control fire
Symbol: Snake

I'm a god with three monster children – the Midgard Serpent, the wolf Fenrir, and the goddess of the underworld, Hel.

Heimdall

The son of Odin, Heimdall was the guardian of the Bifrost bridge that connected Asgard to the rest of the Norse universe. Also known as the "shining god", Heimdall had teeth made of gold.

According to Norse myths, Heimdall would blow the Gjallarhorn [*YAL-ar-horn*] to signal the start of Ragnarök, the final battle.

I need very little sleep and have amazing eyesight and hearing. I can even hear grass grow!

Super facts

Pronunciation: HAME-dahl   **Meaning:** The one who lights the house   **Origin:** Norse mythology   **Location:** North Atlantic and northern Europe   **Other names:** Hallinskiði, Gullintanni, Vindlér or Vindhlér   **Powers:** Foresight, sharp senses, superstrength
Symbols: Bifrost [rainbow bridge], gulltoppr [horse]

Frigg

Wife to Odin and the most important Norse goddess, Frigg was blessed with the power of foresight. This meant she knew the fate of every living thing in the Universe. However, Frigg never shared the information.

My assistants, Fulla and Gna, travelled across the nine Norse worlds to do my bidding.

Frigg was often shown with a spindle, which she used to shape people's destinies.

Super facts

Pronunciation: frig
Meaning: Beloved   **Origin**: Norse mythology
Location: North Atlantic and northern Europe   **Other names**: Frea, Freya, Friia, Frija, Frijjo   **Powers**: Foresight, control over people's destinies
Symbols: Key, ring, spindle, mistletoe

The World Tree

Yggdrasil (*EEG-drass-ill*) was a gigantic tree that sat at the centre of the Norse universe and united the nine worlds around it. These worlds included Midgard, home to humans; Asgard, realm of the gods; and Hel, the underworld. A dragon, a goat, and stags lived and fed on Yggdrasil, putting it in constant danger.

The Dagda

The Dagda was the leader of the Tuatha Dé Danann (*TOO–ha day DAN–an*), a race of godlike beings that once inhabited Ireland. He had many powers and possessions, such as a cauldron that could never be emptied.

The Dagda's club had two ends – one end would kill and the other would bring people back to life.

I own two pigs – one is alive and the other is constantly roasting above a fire, for meat.

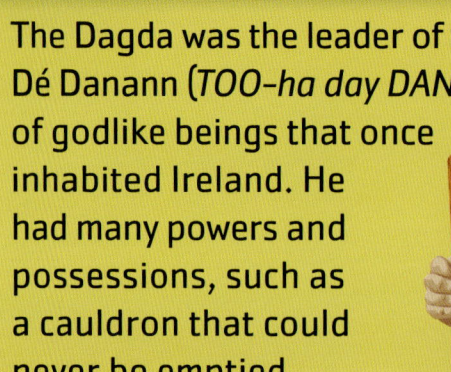

Super facts

Pronunciation: DAH-yuh **Meaning:** The good god
Origin: Celtic mythology **Location:** Northwestern Europe
Other names: Eochaid Ollathair (Eochaid the All-Father),
Ruad Ro-fhessa (Red One of Great Wisdom)
Powers: Ability to give and take life, control over the seasons,
superstrength **Symbols:** Magical cauldron, club, harp

The Morrígan

The Morrígan was an Irish warrior–queen goddess, who was associated with war, death, and the fury of battle. Sometimes known as "Queen of the demons", the Morrígan was the wife of the Dagda.

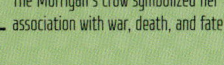

The Morrígan's crow symbolized her association with war, death, and fate.

I am able to take the form of any living animal and often appear as a raven or crow.

Was often shown dressed in red

Super facts

Pronunciation: MOR-i-gan
Meaning: Great queen
Origin: Celtic mythology
Location: Northwestern Europe
Other names: Morrigu, Badbs
Powers: Ability to predict the outcome of battles, shapeshifting, foresight
Symbols: Crow, raven

Brigid

The Celtic goddess of poetry, fertility, and life, Brigid was believed to protect mothers and their newborn children. In Irish myths, Brigid was the daughter of the Dagda.

Was sometimes shown with a fiery halo

I am worshipped on Imbolc, an ancient Celtic festival held on 1 February to celebrate the beginning of spring.

Super facts

Pronunciation: BRIJ-idd
Meaning: Power, vigour, virtue
Origin: Celtic mythology
Location: Northwestern Europe
Other names: Brigantia, Brid, Bride, Briginda, Brigdu, Brigit
Powers: Healing, control over fire and Earth, foresight
Symbols: Fire, holy well, cattle

Rhiannon

Rhiannon, a goddess of Welsh mythology, married King Pwyll (*pooeehl*). However, things weren't always perfect for them. She suffered many misfortunes, including being accused of having her son abducted and then taking his life.

> I didn't kill my son, but I was still unjustly punished.

Super facts

Pronunciation: ree-AN-uhn
Meaning: Great queen
Origin: Welsh and Celtic mythology
Location: Northwestern Europe
Other names: Divine feminine, Night queen
Power: Ability to grant dreams
Symbols: Horses, songbirds, Moon

Rhiannon was often associated with horses, including the pale steed she rode when she first met King Pwyll.

Neit

Super facts

Pronunciation: NAY-t
Meaning: Fighting or passion
Origin: Celtic mythology
Location: Northwestern Europe
Other names: Net, Neith   **Powers:** Skill in battle, power of transformation
Symbols: Sword, shield

Neit, an Irish god of war, was related to a race of giants called the Fomorians. However, during a great battle for Ireland, he sided with the giants' rivals – the Irish gods, called the Tuatha Dé Danann.

> I was killed in battle, but I left many wives and children who later gave birth to the future people of Ireland.

Was usually depicted with weapons and armour

Dea Matrona

Dea Matrona was the Celtic goddess of fertility, nature, and motherhood. She was also worshipped as the goddess of France's River Marne. Many devotees made offerings to her along the river's banks.

Dea Matrona represented fertility and abundance of the natural world.

I was worshipped across the Celtic world, but most strongly in Gaul (modern-day France).

Super facts

Pronunciation: DY-ah ma-TRO-na
Meaning: Divine mother goddess
Origin: Celtic mythology
Location: Northwestern Europe
Other name: Goddess of the Marne
Powers: Life-giving ability, control over water
Symbols: Cornucopia, fruit, bread

Cerridwen

Cerridwen was a Welsh goddess, sorceress, and wife to the giant Tegid Foel (*tee–jid fol*). Together, the couple had a son called Morfran (*mor–frun*), who was said to be the ugliest man in the world.

Super facts

Pronunciation: ke-rid-wen
Meaning: Blessed poetry
Origin: Welsh mythology **Location:** Northwestern Europe
Other names: Cerrydwen, Kerrydwen
Powers: Control over the realms of death, magical abilities, shapeshifting
Symbols: Cauldron, Moon, sow (female pig)

According to Welsh mythology, Cerridwen was the keeper of the cauldron of knowledge.

To make Morfran more appealing, Cerridwen made him the potion of knowledge. But her servant, Gwion (gwi-onn), tasted the potion while stirring it and all its powers went to him.

Did you know?
Cerridwen could shape shift into many animal forms, including a fish, a hawk, and an otter.

Was sometimes depicted in robes of earthly colours, including browns, greens, and greys

Svarog

Svarog was the great Slavic god of blacksmiths, fire, and law. He can be compared to Hephaestus, the Greek god of fire.

> I made the first blacksmith's tongs and weapons. Before that, humans fought with wooden clubs and stones.

Svarog was typically shown with a bushy beard.

Super facts

Pronunciation: sv-a-rog
Meaning: Quarrel, dispute
Origin: Slavic mythology
Location: Eastern and Central Europe, and parts of Asia
Other name: Zuarasici
Powers: Control over fire and metals, power of creation **Symbol:** Slavic svastika (the symbol of the Sun)

Mokosh

In Slavic mythology, Mokosh was the goddess of fertility, the protector of women, and a mother figure. She was also said to watch over sheepshearing, spinning, and weaving.

Super facts

Pronunciation: MOK - osh
Meaning: Moisture
Origin: Slavic mythology
Location: Eastern and Central Europe, and parts of Asia
Other names: Mokosa, Mokosh, Mokusa **Power:** Control over land and agriculture **Symbols:** Sheaves of wheat, spinning wheel

Was usually depicted as a tall woman with long arms

I was found in a cave by the spring god, Jarilo. Together, we made the fruit of the Earth.

Deities of fortune and fate

Many cultures believed their gods and goddesses controlled their destiny and luck in life. Some of these deities decided a person's fate at birth. Others were worshipped to bring about a change in people's fortune.

Fortuna's sacred symbol was a horn of fruit and flowers, called a cornucopia.

Fortune

Goddesses of fortune, such as Lakshmi (*LACK-sh-mee*) from Hindu mythology, could grant good luck and wealth to those who worshipped them. The Roman goddess Fortuna (*for-TYOO-na*) also had the power to bring prosperity and foretell the future.

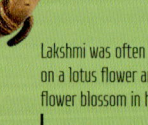

Lakshmi was often shown seated on a lotus flower and holding a flower blossom in her hand.

The Seven Gods of Luck

This group of seven Japanese deities brought happiness and good fortune to people. They travelled together on a treasure ship full of magical objects, including a hat of invisibility and a purse that could never be emptied.

Fate

Goddesses of fate sometimes appeared in threes, like the Greek Clotho [*KLOH-thoh*], Lachesis [*LAK-eh-siss*], and Atropos [*A-tro-poss*], who spun a person's life thread at birth and cut it at death. The Celtic goddess Brigid had the power of prophecy and could glimpse into the future.

Clotho, Lachesis, and Atropos were known as the Moirai by the ancient Greeks, and the Parcae by the Romans.

Brigid was often depicted alongside her two sisters.

Al-Lat

The goddess of war, wellbeing, and prosperity, Al–Lat was worshipped across the ancient Arabian Peninsula, alongside her sisters Manat (*man–nuht*) and Al–Uzza (*al uz–zaa*). The three goddesses were believed to be the daughters of the supreme god.

Super facts

Pronunciation: ahl-laht **Meaning:** Daughter of god
Origin: Arabian mythology **Location:** The Arabian Peninsula
Other names: Allat, Allatu, Alilat
Powers: Control over fertility, seasons, and prosperity **Symbols:** Palm branch, lion

Worshippers built Al-Lat several shrines and temples, including one in Palmyra, Syria. At the temple, there is a statue of the goddess holding a palm branch with a lion at her feet. Travellers prayed to Al-Lat for a safe journey across the desert.

Did you know?
Al-Lat was mentioned by the Greek historian Herodotus in his 5th century BCE work, *Histories*. He said Al-Lat was like the Greek goddess Aphrodite.

The goddess was mostly shown wearing long robes.

Tiamat

To destroy the gods, Tiamat [*tee-uh-mat*] summoned an army of monsters and demons, led by the powerful warrior Qingu [*kin-gwa*]. He carried the Tablet of Destinies that contained the fate of every living thing.

Sharp claws

Tiamat's husband, Apsu, had been plotting to kill his children, but they killed him first.

Feathery tail and body

Tiamat: Creator goddess with a monster army

Battle up!

The Babylonian sea goddess Tiamat was the mother of all gods. When she discovered that her children had killed her husband, Apsu, she vowed to destroy them. Terrified, the gods turned to the great warrior Marduk to stop her.

Marduk was sometimes depicted with wings.

Marduk

The son of the god Ea, Marduk (*mahr-dook*) was born with great strength and wisdom. He offered to fight Tiamat if the gods made him their king. The gods agreed and sent Marduk to fight the goddess.

Marduk was granted control over the four winds when he was young. He made many storms, which annoyed the sea goddess Tiamat.

Marduk: God of thunderstorms

Who wins?

After slaying Tiamat's army, Marduk captured the goddess in his net and shot an arrow through her heart. He then split Tiamat's body in two to create the heavens and the Earth. Finally, Marduk killed Qingu and made human beings from his blood.

Winner!

Enlil

Enlil was the god of wind and nature. It is said that he sent a plague, drought, and flood to wipe out humanity after they angered the gods. However, some people built a boat and survived.

Horned cap

I am one of the main Mesopotamian gods alongside Anu, the father of the gods, and Ea, the god of wisdom.

Super facts

Pronunciation: en-lil
Meaning: Lord wind
Origin: Mesopotamian mythology
Location: Southwestern Asia
Other names: Ellil, Nunamnir
Powers: Control over atmosphere, influence over agriculture   **Symbols:** Thunder and lightning, farming hoe, bull

Ishtar

The Mesopotamian goddess of war and fertility, Ishtar travelled into the underworld and had to strike a deal in order to escape alive. Also known as the "Queen of Heaven", Ishtar was called Inanna by the early Sumerian civilization.

> When I was trapped in the underworld, nothing would grow in the world above.

Ishtar was often depicted wearing beautiful ornaments.

Super facts

Pronunciation: ISH-tar
Meaning: Queen of Heaven
Origin: Mesopotamian mythology
Location: Southwestern Asia
Other name: Inanna
Powers: Control over emotions, fertility, and war **Symbol:** Eight-pointed star

Deities of Ugarit

Ugarit was an ancient city built around 7,000 BCE, in modern–day Syria. Temples and clay tablets discovered in the city show the people living there had a rich mythology and worshipped many gods.

Anat

A goddess of love and war, Anat was admired for her skill in battle. In the Ugarit myths, Anat helped the weather god Baal become king.

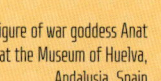

Figure of war goddess Anat at the Museum of Huelva, Andalusia, Spain

Astarte

Astarte [*a-start*] was also a goddess of love and war. She was worshipped by the Hittites, the ancient Indo-European people who lived in what is now modern-day Türkiye (Turkey). She was also known and worshipped across the ancient Middle East, including Canaan and Egypt.

Ugarit artefacts

The city of Ugarit was discovered by accident in 1928. When excavated, it was found to be full of ancient artefacts. These included clay tablets written in an ancient language and gold bowls with images of animals, humans, and gods.

El

El was the supreme god and father of all the Ugarit gods and goddesses, except for Baal. El's wife was Asherah and together the couple created the Universe and everything in it.

Was usually depicted in warrior dress

As god of weather, Baal was usually shown waving thunderbolts.

Baal

The god of weather and fertility, Baal was locked in an eternal struggle with Mot, the god of death and sterility. If Mot defeated Baal, seven years of drought and famine would follow.

Ahura Mazda

In the ancient Persian religion of Zoroastrianism, there were two supreme gods – the wise and kind Ahura Mazda and his wicked brother, Ahriman (*AH–ree–maan*). Ahura Mazda gave humans the power to choose a good path in life, while Ahriman tried to tempt them into evil.

Was usually depicted at the centre of a famous Persian symbol, called Faravahar [*fer-rah-va-har*]

Ahura Mazda and Ahriman were locked in a constant struggle for power. However, in the end, Ahura Mazda triumphed over Ahriman with the help of the god Saoshyant [*soo-shy-ent*].

Super facts

Pronunciation: a-HOO-ra MAZ-da
Meaning: Wise lord   **Origin:** Persian
mythology   **Location:** Persia (modern-day Iran)
Other names: Harzoo, Hormazd, Hourmazd,
Hurmuz, Ohrmazd   **Powers:** Infinite wisdom,
power of creation   **Symbol:** Faravahar
(winged Sun disc)

Did you know?

Ahura Mazda created the
Sun, Moon, stars, and the first
human, called Gayomart.
Ahriman made demons
to destroy his brother's
earthly creations.

Six immortals

In Zoroastrianism, the Amesha Spentas were six immortal beings created by the supreme god Ahura Mazda. The Amesha Spentas helped spread goodness across the human world.

Ameretat

The spirit of immortality, Ameretat [*am-re-taht*] was believed to bless her worshippers with a long life. She was also known as the deity of plants.

Ameretat was most commonly shown in a garden or among shrubs, plants, or trees.

Armaiti

A favourite daughter of Ahura Mazda, Armaiti [*ar-may-tee*] was the spirit of the Earth and the protector of farmers and herdsmen.

Asha

Asha [*ash-ah*], an immortal being associated with fire, was believed to battle evil forces and bring truth and justice to the world.

Was often shown around water or other natural surroundings

Haurvatat

The sister of Ameretat, Haurvatat [*ha-ur-va-taht*] was the spirit of wholeness and perfection. She was also associated with water and good health.

Vohu Manah

The closest god to Ahura Mazda, Vohu Manah [*wa-hoo ma-nah*] ruled over domestic animals, including sheep, dogs, and cattle.

Kshathra Vairya

Ruling over the power of Ahura Mazda's kingdom, Kshathra Vairya [*shuh-tr ve-ryaa*] was the spirit of metal. He was also associated with "good thoughts".

Brahma

In Hindu mythology, Brahma was one of the three creator gods, alongside Vishnu and Shiva. Born from a golden egg or lotus flower, Brahma created the Universe and all living things in it.

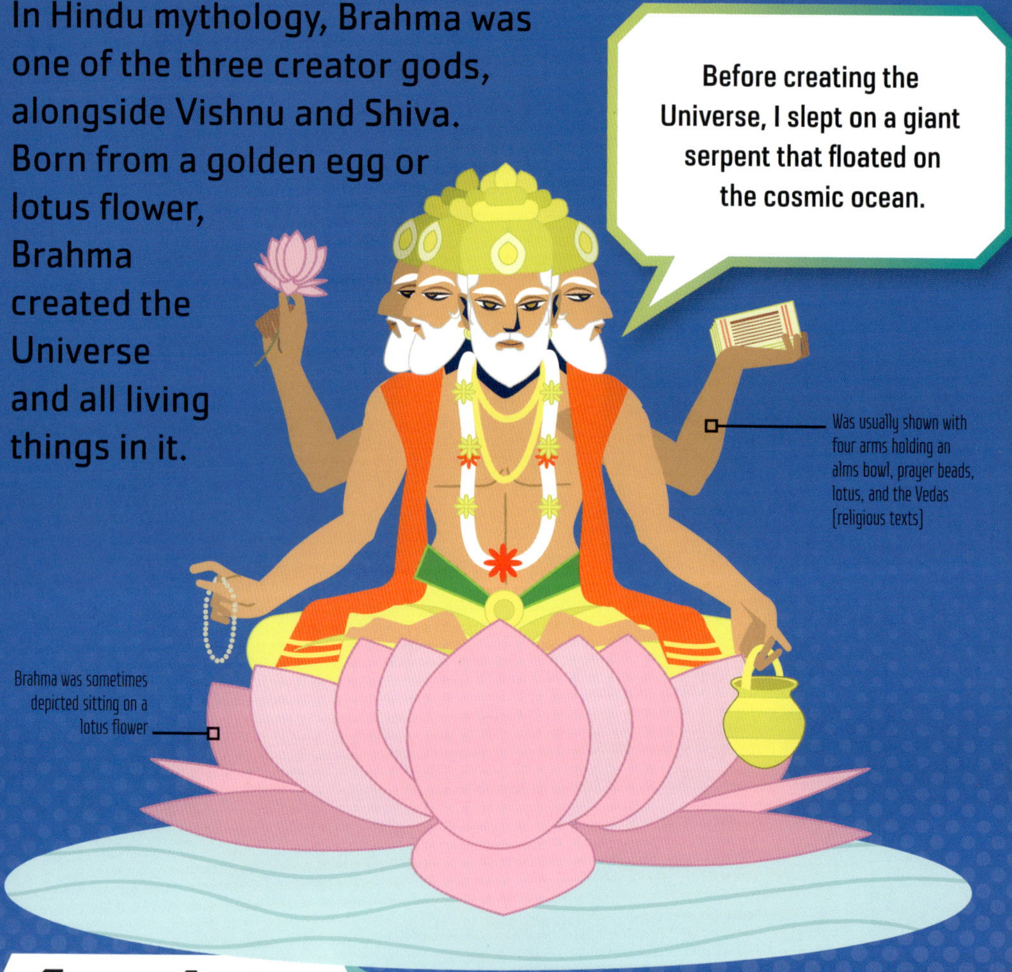

Before creating the Universe, I slept on a giant serpent that floated on the cosmic ocean.

Was usually shown with four arms holding an alms bowl, prayer beads, lotus, and the Vedas (religious texts)

Brahma was sometimes depicted sitting on a lotus flower

Super facts

Pronunciation: BRAH-ma   **Meaning:** Creator of the Universe
Origin: Hindu mythology   **Location:** South Asia
Other names: Svayambhu, Virinchi, Prajapati
Powers: Immense knowledge, life-giving ability, control over time
Symbols: Lotus, Vedas (religious texts), japamala (prayer beads), swan

Vishnu

A chief deity, Vishnu was the preserver and protector of the Universe. He was believed to return to Earth to defeat the forces of evil and restore order.

Super facts

Pronunciation: vish-noo
Meaning: One who is everything and inside everything **Origin:** Hindu mythology **Location:** South Asia
Other names: Narayana, Hari
Powers: Ability to see and know everything in the Universe, power to take human forms
Symbols: Discus, lotus, conch shell, mace

I have been reincarnated (reborn) nine times! I've come back as a fish, turtle, and boar.

Vishnu was usually shown lying back on the coils of a multiheaded serpent.

Shiva

One of the three most important Hindu gods, alongside Brahma and Vishnu, Shiva was known as "The Destroyer". This is because he destroyed evil when it threatened the world.

Super facts

Pronunciation: SHI-vah
Meaning: The auspicious one
Origin: Hindu mythology **Location:** South Asia
Other names: Mahesha, Mahadeva, Shambhu
Powers: Third eye (the source of immense energy that destroys evil), ability to create, transform, and destroy the world **Symbols:** Third eye, cobra, sacred ash, trident

The cobra around Shiva's neck signified power over the world's most dangerous creatures.

Shiva took many different forms, including the half-man and half-woman form (called Ardhanarishvara). Split equally down the middle, Ardhanarishvara showed Shiva on one side and his wife, Parvati, on the other.

He was shown with three eyes, including one on his forehead.

The three-pronged trident represented the three Hindu gods – Shiva, Brahma, and Vishnu.

Did you know?
Shiva was depicted wearing animal skins, symbolizing his connection to the wild. He was often surrounded by simple, natural elements.

Mahishasura

In his quest for immortality, Mahishasura [*MA-he-SHA-sur-a*] struck a deal with the god Brahma that he could not be killed by any god or mortal man. Mahishasura then began attacking everyone in heaven and on Earth. Could he be stopped?

This half-bull, half-man demon was often shown with horns.

Called the "Buffalo demon", Mahishasura could take the form of a buffalo, or a man, or half of each!

A spear granted by the god of fire

Usually wore gold ornaments

Mahishasura: Power-hungry buffalo demon

Battle up!

Mahishasura was a shapeshifting asura (demon) from Hindu mythology. He sought victory over the devas (gods), who were the sworn enemies of the asuras. Mahishasura led a battle against the gods to force them out of their heavenly home.

Durga

Durga had 10 arms and each held a powerful weapon.

As Mahishasura could not be defeated by any god or man, only a woman could banish him. The Hindu gods Vishnu, Brahma, and Shiva created a great flame, from which emerged the warrior goddess Durga (*dur-gah*), ready to fight Mahishasura.

Durga was said to be more powerful than Vishnu, Brahma, and Shiva put together. She often rode a lion into battle.

Durga: Demon-slaying warrior goddess

Who wins?

With weapons held high in her 10 hands, Durga rode in on a lion to attack Mahishasura. The demon fought back by transforming into an elephant and a buffalo. The battle raged for hours, but Durga finally defeated Mahishasura by beheading him.

Winner!

Pángǔ

In Chinese mythology, Pángǔ was a hairy, horned creator god who spent 18,000 years growing inside a cosmic egg. He finally hatched from the egg to form the Universe.

He used his huge axe to separate the heavens from the Earth.

Super facts

Pronunciation: pahn-GOO   **Meaning:** Ancient dome
Origin: Chinese mythology   **Location:** East Asia
Other names: Pa Kua, P'an Ku, P'an K'uei
Powers: Power of creation, superstrength
Symbols: Yin yang (symbol depicting two opposite forces, like light and dark), tortoise, crane (bird)

After Pángǔ finished making the Universe, he died and his body became the mountains, soil, and stars. The goddess Nǔ wā (*nyoo-wah*), shown here as part serpent, then made the first human beings.

Pángǔ's cosmic egg was the first object to be formed at the beginning of time.

Did you know?
Pángǔ was also sometimes depicted as a dwarf covered with leaves.

Primordial emperors

The Jade Emperor was the Chinese god who created the world. After doing so, he realized that the growing number of people needed guidance. He then created three primordial emperors, who acted like governors, to help humans. The emperors taught them skills and gave knowledge to live peacefully.

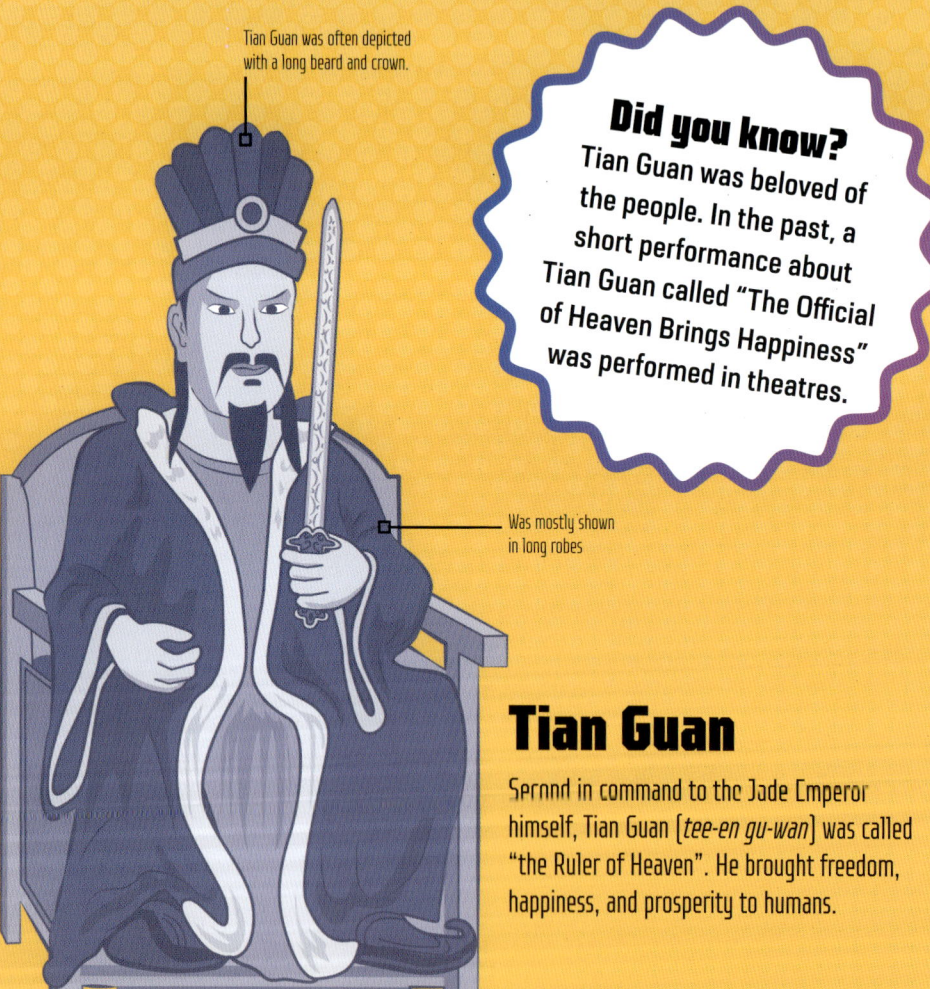

Tian Guan was often depicted with a long beard and crown.

Was mostly shown in long robes

Did you know?
Tian Guan was beloved of the people. In the past, a short performance about Tian Guan called "The Official of Heaven Brings Happiness" was performed in theatres.

Tian Guan

Second in command to the Jade Emperor himself, Tian Guan (*tee-en gu-wan*) was called "the Ruler of Heaven". He brought freedom, happiness, and prosperity to humans.

The Jade Emperor

The Jade Emperor was the ruler of heaven. Also called Shang Di, meaning "Lord of Heaven", he was believed to be an important god who watched over everything from the heavens above.

Di Guan

Called "the Ruler of Earth", Di Guan [*dee gu-wan*] was the primordial emperor who judged people's actions and could forgive their sins.

Shui Guan was almost always shown alongside Di Guan and Tian Guan.

Shui Guan

Also known as "The Ruler of the Waters", Shui Guan [*sh-way gu-wan*] showed humans how to farm, drain water, prevent floods, and avoid misfortune.

The legend of the Ten Suns

In Chinese mythology, ten suns took turns shining on the Earth. Once they all appeared together in the sky, making the Earth unbearably hot. The chief god then sent the archer Hòu Yì (*ho-yee*) to Earth. He shot down nine of the suns from the sky, leaving behind the one Sun we have today.

Izanagi

One of the 16 creator gods, Izanagi used a spear to pull up Japan's first island from the primordial ocean. It was believed that the Moon, the Sun, and storm gods were born from his eyes and nose.

My wife, goddess Izanami, died after giving birth to Kagutsuchi, the fire god.

Izanagi's spear was called Amenonuhoko [*ame-nonu-hoko*].

Super facts

Pronunciation: ee-zah-nah-gee
Meaning: He who invites
Origin: Japanese mythology   **Location:** East Asia
Other name: Izanagi no Mikoto   **Power:** Power of creation
Symbol: Powerful spear

Izanami

After Izanami died, Izanagi travelled to the underworld to get her back. But after seeing her decaying body, Izanagi rushed away in horror. He blocked the underworld's doorway behind him, sealing in his wife forever. Izanami then became the Japanese goddess of death.

> After the first Japanese island was formed, I gave birth to its trees, mountains, seas, and rivers – each with its own type of god.

Izanami was shown as a young woman wearing a traditional Japanese kimono.

Super facts

Pronunciation: ee-zah-nah-mee
Meaning: She who invites **Origin:** Japanese mythology **Location:** East Asia **Other name:** Izanami no Mikoto **Power:** Power of creation
Symbols: Powerful spear, weaving tools

She shared the spear with Izanagi.

Amaterasu

The Shinto Sun goddess Amaterasu was born from the eye of the creator god, Izanagi. He told the dazzling Amaterasu to move into the sky so she didn't scorch the Earth.

Amaterasu was often depicted with a shining solar disc on her head.

After I moved into the sky to warm the world, I showed the humans below how to grow rice.

Super facts

Pronunciation: a-ma-teh-RA-soo
Meaning: Shining in heaven
Origin: Japanese mythology
Location: East Asia   **Other names:** Amaterasu-ōmikami, Ōhirume-no-muchi-no-kami   **Powers:** Control over light, authority over spirits   **Symbols:** Sun, mirror

Susanoo

The Shinto storm god Susanoo was born when Izanagi blew his nose! However, he behaved badly towards his sister, Amaterasu, and damaged her rice fields. For this, Susanoo was thrown out of heaven.

> On Earth, I killed an eight-headed dragon and married Princess Kushinadahime (*koo-shee-nah-dah-hee-meh*), whom I had rescued.

Used his legendary sword, Kusanagi, to slay the eight-headed dragon

Super facts

Pronunciation: su-sa-no-o
Meaning: Reckless   **Origin:** Japanese mythology   **Location:** East Asia
Other names: Takehaya-Susanoo-no-Mikoto, Haya-Susanoo-no-Mikoto
Powers: Conjuring and controlling storms and lightning, superstrength
Symbols: Lightning, storms, sea

Inari

Super facts

Pronunciation: ee-nar-ee
Meaning: Rice carrier
Origin: Japanese mythology
Location: East Asia
Other names: Ukanomitama no Kami, Ukemochi no Kami
Powers: Control over fortune, great cunning   **Symbol:** Fox

Inari was the Japanese deity of foxes, fertility, rice, agriculture and industry, and general prosperity. They were sometimes represented as male, and other times as female. Two foxes were said to serve as Inari's messengers on Earth.

Inari sometimes appeared as a beautiful, young woman.

I am such a popular deity that more than 30,000 shrines were built for me across Japan.

Kagutsuchi

Kagutsuchi was the fearsome god of fire. At the time of his birth, he accidentally set his mother, Izanami, alight. Izanami's death angered Kagutsuchi's father, who then beheaded him.

Kagutsuchi was often depicted as a fiery being, constantly emitting intense flames.

After my early death, pieces of my body turned into several gods and volcanoes.

Super facts

Pronunciation: Kah-GOO-tschee   **Meaning**: He who starts fires   **Origin**: Japanese mythology   **Location**: East Asia
Other names: Hi-no-Kagutsuchi, Kagutsuchi-no-kami, Homusubi
Power: Control over fire   **Symbols**: Volcanoes, fire

Mireuk

Mireuk was the Korean creator god who separated the Earth from the heavens, and gave fire and water to the world. He transformed two caterpillars into the first humans and taught them to feed and clothe themselves.

Super facts

Pronunciation: mee-ruhk   **Meaning:** Future Buddha
Origin: Korean mythology   **Location:** East Asia
Other names: Maitreya, Sakyamuni Buddha
Powers: Power of creation, unparalleled wisdom, ability to maintain balance and harmony in the Universe
Symbols: Pagoda (sacred building), dragon flower tree

After Mireuk filled the world with good things, the evil god Seokga (*sok-ka*), seen here, challenged him to a flower-growing contest. Mireuk grew the best flower, but Seokga stole it and claimed control of the world. For the first time, the world was filled with suffering and misery.

Did you know?
Mireuk paid a mouse with rice for showing him where to find fire and water. It is thought this is why mice are always able to secretly steal rice from people.

Mireuk was sometimes shown as a small, stout man.

Haemosu

In Korean mythology, Haemosu was the Sun god and son of the Celestial Emperor. Every morning, Haemosu rode his chariot down to Earth and every evening back to heaven. This represented sunrise and sunset.

Often wore a headdress made of crow feathers

As the god of the Sun, I symbolize light and power.

Super facts

Pronunciation: HAY-mo-soo
Meaning: God of the Sun
Origin: Korean mythology
Location: East Asia
Other name: Cheonwangrang
Powers: Control over the Sun and agriculture, archery
Symbols: Sun, golden chariot, dragons

Dalnim

As the goddess of the Moon, Dalnim controlled the tides on the Earth and provided comfort to people who were lost or in trouble. She also guided the souls of the dead to the afterlife.

Was often depicted with the Moon

Super facts

Pronunciation: dahl-neem

Meaning: Moon

Origin: Korean mythology

Location: East Asia

Other name: Dalsun

Powers: Control over tides, can find paths and guide lost souls

Symbols: Moon, rabbit

Travellers believe I watch over them from above and keep them safe.

Egyptian deities

During their long history, the ancient Egyptians worshipped hundreds of gods and goddesses. These gods had many forms, names, and roles. While some became less or more important as time went on, all of them originally emerged from the same endless sea.

Ra

Ra was the Sun god and the king of all Egyptian gods. It is said that he crossed the sky every day and passed through the underworld every night.

Many depictions of Ra showed him as a man with a hawk's head.

Shu

Shu was the god of air and father to Geb and Nut. Ra commanded Shu to keep his children apart, so there would be space between the Earth and sky.

The ankh, a type of cross, is a symbol of life.

Nut

Nut was goddess of the sky who sometimes took the form of a cow. Nut was often shown as a woman with a long back, bent over the Earth below her.

Tefnut

The goddess of moisture and rainfall, Tefnut was the wife and sister of Shu. Tefnut was depicted as a woman with the head of a lioness.

Geb

Geb was the Earth god who held the world together with his body. He was the son of Shu and was often depicted alongside his father.

The goose, Geb's sacred symbol, was often shown on his head.

Sometimes Tefnut was shown to carry a sceptre.

Osiris

First king of Egypt, Osiris was its most beloved god. He travelled the Earth teaching humans how to grow crops. But his jealous brother Set killed him by cutting his body into 14 pieces.

Set never forgave me for leaving Isis, my wife, in charge of the kingdom instead of him, when I went travelling.

Was often depicted with green skin

Super facts

Pronunciation: oh-SAI-riss **Meaning:** Powerful, mighty **Origin:** Egyptian mythology
Location: Egypt and northeastern Africa
Other names: Wennefer, Khentiamenti
Powers: Power over the dead as a resurrected king, control over agriculture and afterlife
Symbols: Crook, flail, mummy, Atef crown

Isis

Isis often wore a solar disc as a headdress.

The Egyptian goddess Isis was shocked when she learned her husband was dead. With the help of Anubis, the god of the afterlife, she put his body back together and breathed life into him. They then created Horus (*HOR–uss*), who fought against Set.

After saving Osiris, I became a great magician. Osiris, however, did not survive and went on to become the god of Duat, the Egyptian underworld.

Super facts

Pronunciation: AI-siss
Meaning: Queen of the throne
Origin: Egyptian mythology
Location: Egypt and northeastern Africa
Other name: Aset
Powers: Healing power, magical abilities
Symbols: Ankh, sistrum (rattle), Isis knot

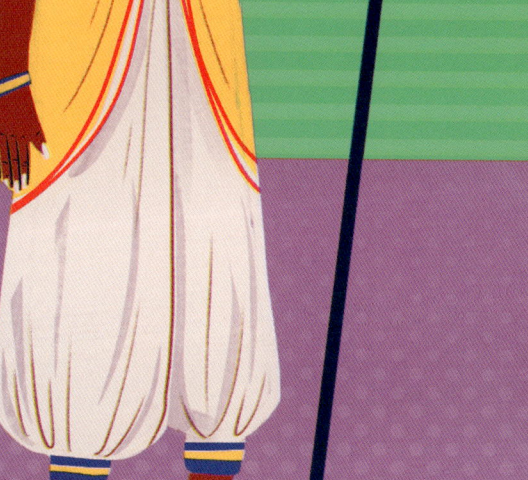

Horus was often shown with the head of a falcon and the body of a human.

Horus

When Set challenged Horus to a breath-holding competition for the throne, as rightful king, Horus accepted. Both of them changed into hippopotamuses and submerged themselves in the River Nile. However, the competition ended when Isis harpooned them both.

After Isis harpooned Horus, he cut off her head! She was reborn, but Horus hid away in shame.

Horus: Vengeful son of Osiris

Battle up!

The son of Osiris and Isis, Horus was determined to defeat the evil god Set, who had killed his father. But Set would not give up his new position as king of the gods and a long war between the two began.

Set was depicted with the head of a dog and a long snout.

Set

After the competition, Horus went into hiding. But Set found Horus sleeping beneath a tree and poked out his eyes. Later, the goddess Hathor (*HA-thor*) restored Horus's sight by pouring milk onto his wounds.

During this war, Set was able to win some gods over by telling them lies about Horus.

Set: God of chaos, storms, and disorder

Who wins?

To settle their war, Horus and Set agreed to race stone boats down the River Nile. But Horus secretly made his boat of wood, while Set's stone boat simply sank. Furious, Set turned into a hippopotamus and attacked Horus's boat. Exhausted by the ongoing war, Osiris ruled that Horus would become king of the gods.

Winner!

The eternal battle

The Egyptian god of darkness and disorder, Apep was a monstrous serpent who tried to devour the Sun god Ra and prevent his journey across the sky. But every day, Ra defeated Apep and the Sun would shine on the Earth once more. This battle symbolized the eternal fight of light and order against darkness and chaos.

Mawu

Mawu was the creator goddess from Gbe folklore. At the beginning of time, she created the gods of the sky and Earth, and then the world and its people.

> I rode on the back of the serpent Aido-Hwedo, and together we created the Universe and its elements.

It is said that the Earth's landscape was shaped by the serpent Aido-Hwedo.

Super facts

Pronunciation: maa-woo
Meaning: Sky, rain
Origin: Gbe mythology
Location: West Africa
Other names: Mawu-Lisa, Mahu
Powers: Power of creation, life-giving ability **Symbols:** Moon, Earth, serpent, water

Olodumare

The Yoruba people of West Africa believed that Olodumare was the supreme spirit, the lord of heaven, and the creator god. He turned the Earth from a marshy wasteland into a solid ball.

Olodumare stood at the centre of the Universe and created the Earth and other planets around him.

Heaven used to be closer to the Earth, but I raised it higher when humans began wiping their hands on the sky.

Ananse

Ananse was the shapeshifting trickster–hero of West African folklore. Powerful and super clever, Ananse taught humans how to write and then gave them all the wisdom and knowledge in the world.

Ananse normally appeared as a spider, but he could also change into a human form.

I once tricked the sky god, Nyame, into making me the King of All Wisdom.

Super facts

Pronunciation: an-AN-see **Meaning:** Spider
Origin: Akan mythology **Location:** West Africa
Other names: Anansi, Anancy, Kwaku
Powers: Ability to transform his weaknesses into strength, power to outsmart his opponents
Symbol: Spider web

Nyame

Nyame was the sky god and Supreme Being of Akan folklore. Nyame created the Earth for humans to live on, and then sent his four sons to show people how to hunt, farm, and live well.

Super facts

Pronunciation: n-ay-AH-m-ee
Meaning: He who knows and sees everything   **Origin:** Akan mythology
Location: West Africa
Other names: Nyambe, Nyankopon, Onyame   **Powers:** Influence over natural elements, life-giving ability
Symbol: Nyame Dua (God's Tree)

I once sent a goat to tell humans that they would die one day, and then journey to the sky to join me in heaven.

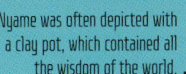
Nyame was often depicted with a clay pot, which contained all the wisdom of the world.

89

Bull ritual of Mithra

In Mithraism (a Persian religion), during the creation of the world, the Sun god ordered the deity Mithra (*mith-ra*) to slay a cosmic bull. Mithra was saddened by this task, but when he slit the bull's throat, a miracle occurred. From the bull's blood came wheat, wine, and the seeds that later created every creature on Earth.

91

Viracocha

Viracocha was a chief Inca god who created people, other gods, and the Earth, Sun, and Moon. He then travelled the world to teach people how to farm and also gave them clothing, language, animals, and art.

Super facts

Pronunciation: vee-rah-KOH-chah
Meaning: Lake or sea foam **Origin:** Inca mythology
Location: Western South America **Other names:** Tunupa, Wiraqucha Pachayachachiq **Powers:** Power of creation, unparalleled wisdom, shapeshifting, control over nature
Symbols: Sceptre, Chakana (Andean Cross)

The Inca believed that Viracocha emerged from Lake Titicaca, and created the Earth and heavens on its shore. This ancient lake, shared by Peru and Bolivia, is South America's largest freshwater lake.

Feathered headdress

Did you know?
Disguised, Viracocha passed on knowledge to people. But after seeing the evil of humankind, he drowned them in a flood.

Viracocha was often shown with a sceptre, a symbol of authority.

Gitchi Manitou

Gitchi Manitou is a North American creator god worshipped by the Anishinaabe (*ah-nish-ih-NAH-bay*) peoples. They believe he gave life to Earth's plants and animals, before creating people.

Sometimes called the supreme being

I created a family for the young Earth with the Moon, called grandmother, and the Sun, called grandfather.

Super facts

Pronunciation: gi-chee muh-nih-doo   **Meaning:** Great spirit
Origin: Folklore of Indigenous peoples of the Pacific Northwest
Location: North America   **Other name:** Kitchi Manitou
Powers: Power of creation

Dayuni'si

According to the folklore of Indigenous peoples of the Pacific Northwest, Dayuni'si is a creator god who became a water beetle to build the world. He made the Earth from the mud he stirred up from the seafloor.

Super facts

Pronunciation: da-yoo-nee-see
Meaning: Beaver's grandchild, water beetle **Origin:** Folklore of Indigenous peoples of the Pacific Northwest
Location: North America
Other names: Dâyuni'sï, Water beetle
Powers: Shapeshifting, power of creation

I was born into the sky realm, but wanted to see if anything lay below the vast sea that covered the world below.

Dayuni'si is often shown in the water beetle form he took to create the Earth.

Sun Dance

The Sun Dance is an annual ceremony performed by Indigenous peoples of the Pacific Northwest. People meet for rituals before putting up a central pole, then dance to celebrate the Universe. This can sometimes go on for several days in a row.

Ukko

The god of thunder, Ukko was one of the most important figures in Finnish mythology. Because he was believed to control rainfall, sacrifices were made to Ukko during crop planting and in times of drought.

Was often depicted with lightning bolts

Super facts

Pronunciation: OO-ko   **Meaning:** Thunder, old man
Origin: Finnish mythology   **Location:** Finland
Other name: Jumala   **Powers:** Control over thunder and rainfall, influence over the fertility of land
Symbols: Golden club, hammer, axe, sword, arrow

During wartime, Finnish warriors often prayed to Ukko for protection. They believed he could provide magical charms that would safeguard them from the enemy.

Ukko's hammer was called Ukonvasara [*OO-kon-vah-sah-rah*].

Did you know?
Ukko's name comes from the Finnish word "Ukkonen", which means both "thunder" and "old man".

Quetzalcōātl

Known as "The Plumed Serpent", Quetzalcōātl was the Aztec creator god who made the world and humans. He then gave people maize (corn), the main crop grown by the Aztecs.

Super facts

Pronunciation: keht-sahl-koh-ahtl
Meaning: Feathered serpent
Origin: Aztec mythology
Location: Central and southern Mexico
Other names: White Tezcatlipoca, Precious Twin, Tlahuizcalpantecuhtli **Powers**: Life-giving ability, flight, control over rain, winds, and storms **Symbols**: Snake, crow, macaw

Ehecatl (*e-HE-kah-tl*) was the Aztec god of wind and rain, worshipped as Quetzalcōātl in another form. He was therefore often called Quetzalcōātl-Ehecatl.

Quetzalcōātl was typically shown with a conical hat called a copilli.

Was usually depicted wearing the feathers of the green quetzal bird

Did you know?
Quetzalcōātl once travelled to the underworld to collect human bones to make more people with.

Huītzilōpōchtli

God of the Sun and war, Huītzilōpōchtli was one of the most important Aztec gods. Born to the Earth goddess Coatlicue, Huītzilōpōchtli fought and killed his siblings. He then guided the Aztecs to their capital of Tenochtitlan in modern–day Mexico.

His helmet was made of hummingbird feathers.

Huītzilōpōchtli used a fire serpent, Xiuhcóatl, as his weapon.

I was conceived in my mother's womb when she seized hummingbird feathers falling from the sky.

Super facts

Pronunciation: hyut-zi-luh-paw-cht-lee
Meaning: Hummingbird of the south
Origin: Aztec mythology **Location:** Central and southern Mexico
Other names: Xiuhpilli (Turquoise Prince), Totec (Our Lord)
Powers: Superstrength, wielding a fire serpent
Symbols: Hummingbird, eagle, Sun

Tēzcatlīpohca

Tēzcatlīpohca was the Aztec god of the night who could see everything in the world – including the thoughts of humans – in his obsidian mirror. Tēzcatlīpohca rewarded good deeds with riches and fame, and punished wrongdoers with sickness and poverty.

Super facts

Pronunciation: tez-ca-tlee-POH-ka
Meaning: Smoking mirror
Origin: Aztec mythology
Location: Central and southern Mexico
Other names: Ehécatl (Night Wind), Yaotl (Warrior), Telpochtli (Young Man)
Powers: Shapeshifting, power to destroy the sky
Symbols: Smoking mirror, jaguar, eagle

He was often depicted in a warrior's attire.

My obsidian mirror could reveal the true nature of people.

Obsidian mirror in place of one of his feet

103

Itzamná

An important Maya deity, Itzamná was the god of heaven, as well as day and night. He taught humans about medicine, the arts, and the written word.

Itzamná was usually depicted as a wise old man with no teeth and sunken cheeks.

> I sometimes take the form of a massive, two-headed serpent, which represents the Milky Way.

Super facts

Pronunciation: eetz-am-NAH
Meaning: Wise person **Origin:** Maya mythology
Location: Central America
Other names: Kukulcan, Itzam Cab Ain
Powers: Shapeshifting, healing, divination
Symbols: Two-headed underwater serpent, caiman

Gucumatz

With the body of a long, feathered serpent, Gucumatz was the Maya god of life, creation, and nature. He was believed to rule over weather and storms, so was responsible for a good harvest.

Super facts

Pronunciation: goo-coo-matz
Meaning: Feathered serpent
Origin: Maya mythology
Location: Central America
Other name: Q'uq'umatz
Powers: Control over rain, power to bring balance to the world
Symbols: Feathered serpent, Sun, sky

My earthly part-snake and part-feathered bird form signifies connection between land and sky.

The yellow, green, and blue colours represent life and the natural world.

105

Atabey

Super facts

Pronunciation: ah-tah-bay
Meaning: Father prince   **Origin:** Taíno mythology   **Location:** Caribbean and Florida   **Other name:** Atabek
Powers: Life-giving power of the Earth, power to bring springs of fresh water, authority over the fertility of the land
Symbols: Earth, fresh water

According to the mythology of the Caribbean Taíno people, Atabey was one of the two supreme deities. She represented the Earth, fresh water, and fertility.

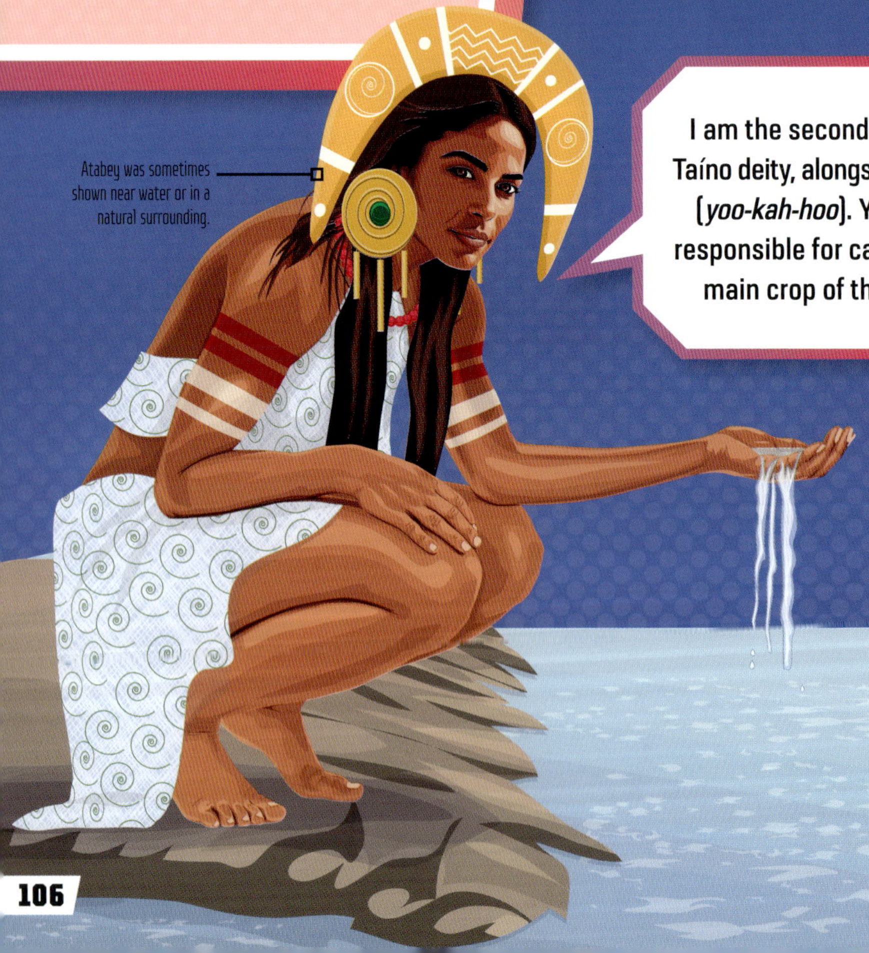

Atabey was sometimes shown near water or in a natural surrounding.

I am the second supreme Taíno deity, alongside Yucahu (*yoo-kah-hoo*). Yucahu is responsible for cassava, the main crop of the Taíno.

Guabancex

Guabancex was the bad–tempered Taíno deity of hurricanes. It was said that Guabancex's fury created terrible storms that swept across the Caribbean, destroying everything in her path.

Guabancex was shown with S-shaped arms and an angry face.

Sometimes I work with three minor deities, who control rain, thunder, and lightning. Together, we make the most ferocious storms.

Super facts

Pronunciation: gwah-ban-seks
Meaning: Mother of storms, hurricane bringer
Origin: Taíno mythology   **Location:** Caribbean and Florida
Power: Control over storms and natural disasters
Symbols: Storms, clay jars

Inti

Inti was the Inca sky and Sun god who warmed up the land every day with his rays. Inti sent his children down to Earth to start the Inca civilization.

I helped the first Incan ruler, Manco Capac, find the best place to build his capital city of Cuzco.

Init was usually depicted wearing gold ornaments as his sweat was believed to be gold.

Super facts

Pronunciation: In-tee
Meaning: Sun   **Origin:** Inca mythology
Location: Western South America
Other names: Apu Inti, Apu Punchau, Punchau
Powers: Power over the Sun, control over weather, military skill
Symbols: Gold statue, Sun disc, golden mask

Pachamama

Inca Earth goddess and mother to Inti, Pachamama was known as the mother of mountains. She could cause earthquakes if she was disrespected. Farmers made offerings to her for a bountiful harvest.

Super facts

Pronunciation: PA-cha-ma-ma
Meaning: Mother Earth
Origin: Inca mythology
Location: Western South America
Other names: Earth Mother, Pacha
Powers: Power of creation, control over life and death
Symbols: Old woman, spiral, bowl of dirt

On 1 August each year, farmers offer food and drink to me. They bury them in a hole in the ground to express their gratitude.

Was shown as being part of the Earth, mountains, and nature

Rainbow Serpent

The Rainbow Serpent is the creator-deity from First Australian folklore. Some say it created Australia's mountains and valleys by pushing upwards from under the ground. Others think the serpent carved out the landscape by dragging its long body across the land.

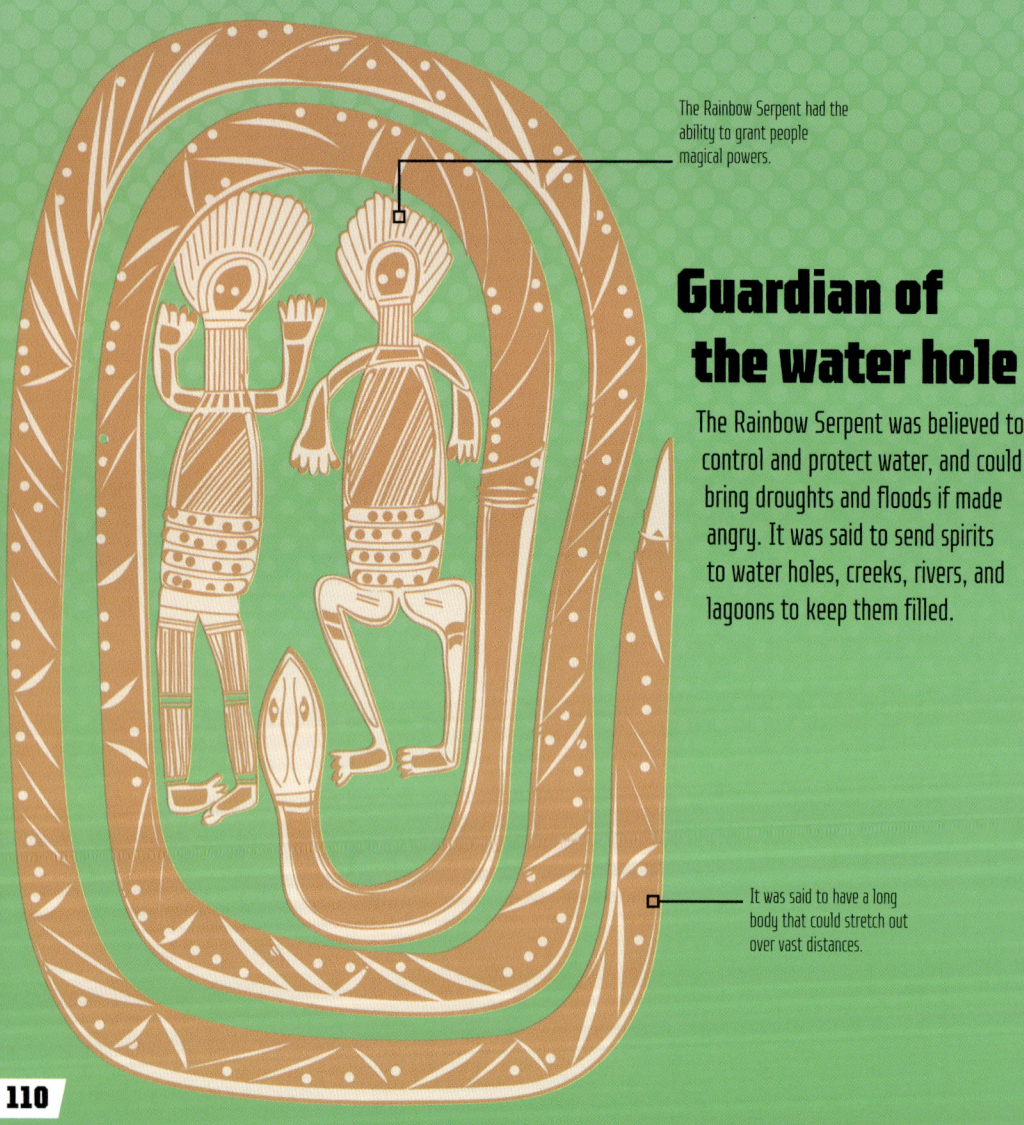

The Rainbow Serpent had the ability to grant people magical powers.

Guardian of the water hole

The Rainbow Serpent was believed to control and protect water, and could bring droughts and floods if made angry. It was said to send spirits to water holes, creeks, rivers, and lagoons to keep them filled.

It was said to have a long body that could stretch out over vast distances.

Taipan

The deadly Australian taipan is sometimes associated with the Rainbow Serpent. The large, fast-moving snake is highly venomous and can leap off the ground to bite its victim.

At the end of the rainbow

The First Australian peoples believe that a rainbow in the sky is in fact the Rainbow Serpent. It's thought that the rainbow is the serpent travelling from one water hole to another, making sure they stay full and don't dry up.

Paying respect

Today some First Australian communities practise rituals for the Rainbow Serpent. They show it respect through rituals before approaching a water hole.

Pele

Super facts

Pronunciation: PEH-lay
Meaning: The woman who devours the land
Origin: Hawaiian mythology
Location: The Hawaiian Islands
Other name: Ka wahine'ai honua
Powers: Control over fire and lava, volcanic eruptions   **Symbol:** Volcanoes

The Hawaiian goddess of fire and volcanoes, Pele was responsible for creating new lands and also destroying them. When angered, she would unleash volcanic eruptions and lava.

I am both feared and respected – my eruptions can bring death and destruction but also new land, once the lava has cooled.

When in human form, Pele was often shown as a woman.

Tangaroa

Tangaroa was worshipped by Polynesian cultures as the god of creation and the ocean. In Māori mythology, Tangaroa's offspring became the first fish in the sea.

> As the ocean god, I control the tides, the waves, and the storms at sea.

Super facts

Pronunciation: tongue-a-roar-ah
Meaning: God of the sea
Origin: Māori mythology
Location: Polynesian islands
Other name: Tangaroa-whakamautai
Powers: Control over ocean, superstrength
Symbols: Sea, ocean, marine life

When depicted as a human, his skin was the colour of the deep ocean.

Hina

Hina was the Polynesian goddess of beauty and the Moon, ocean, and sea creatures. In Māori mythology, Hina was thought to be either the older sister or the wife of the Polynesian demigod Māui (*MOW–ee*).

> I once showed Māui how to plait my hair into a rope to snare the Sun and make the days longer.

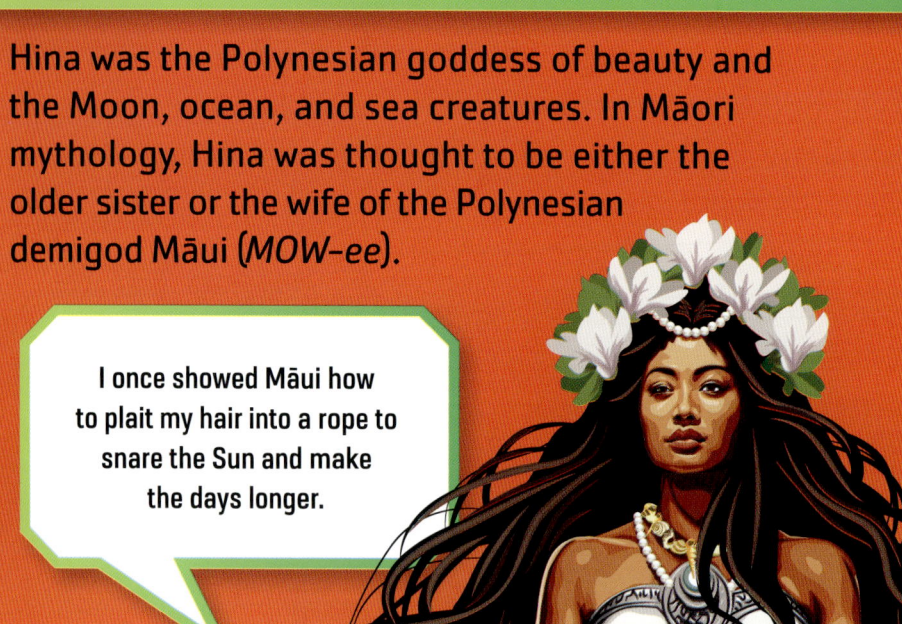

Long hair

Was usually shown wearing traditional Polynesian dress

Super facts

Pronunciation: HEE-na **Meaning**: Sunlight, greenery **Origin**: Māori mythology
Location: Polynesian islands **Other names**: Hina, Sina, Hine, Ina **Power**: Control over ocean and seasons **Symbols**: Moon, jasmine

Papatūānuku

In Māori mythology, Papatūānuku was both the earth mother and the land. She gave birth to all living things, including plants, trees and people. Her husband was Ranginui (*ran–gi–NOO–ee*), the sky.

> Ranginui used to be close enough to touch me, until Māui and his brothers pushed us apart.

Papatūānuku was said to be draped in a grand feather cloak.

Super facts

Pronunciation: pa-pa-too-a-NOO-koo **Meaning:** Earth mother
Origin: Māori mythology **Location:** Polynesian islands
Other names: Papa, Nuku **Powers:** Control over land and nature, power of creation **Symbols:** Earth, river, flowers

Afterlife

Every culture has a story about what happens after death. Many believe in some form of afterlife. While some see it as a paradise, others think of it as a place of judgement and punishment.

P'an Kuan is usually depicted in traditional Chinese dress, wielding a sword.

Patala

The Hindu underworld Patala [*pa-tah-al*] is made up of seven realms, which are thought to be below the Earth. The seventh and lowest realm is the Patala loka.

Patala loka is the region of the semi-divine serpents, called nagas.

Dìyù

The Chinese underworld Dìyù [*dee-yoo*] is a place of judgement and P'an Kuan [*paan-gwaan*] is a judge. He would consider each person's behaviour on Earth before deciding on their eternal fate.

Elysium

In ancient Greek mythology, the afterlife is called Elysium (*eh-LI-zee-um*) – a paradise of perfect happiness with no problems. It started as a place only for heroes, but later, mortals who had lived a good life could also enter.

Also called the Elysian Fields, Elysium is a paradise of beautiful, green meadows.

Valkyrie carrying a fallen soldier to Valhalla

Mictlán

Mictlán (*MEEK-t-laan*) is the nine-levelled Aztec land of the dead. It takes years for the deceased to journey through its levels, crossing a field of flesh-scraping knives and a river of blood to get there.

Valhalla

Valhalla is the great hall of Norse god Odin and the destination for warriors who had died heroically on the battlefield. In Valhalla, the dead warriors prepare for the last battle, called Ragnarök.

Winged creatures

From fire-breathing dragons and flying horses to man-eating birds and riddle-speaking sphinxes, there is a multitude of mythological winged creatures. These masters of the sky can beat their wings to cause thunderclaps, light up the night with glowing feathers, or soar across land and sea at lightning speed.

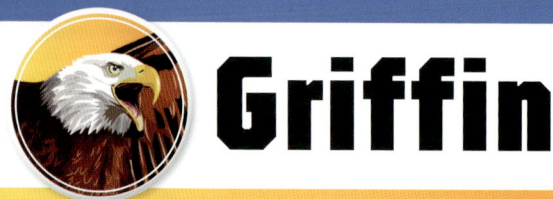

Griffin

Super facts

Pronunciation: GRIF-in
Origin: Greek mythology
Location: Greece and western coast of Türkiye (Turkey) **Characteristics:** Head and front legs of an eagle, back legs and tail of a lion **Lookalikes:** Lamassu (Mesopotamian), Tiamat (Babylonian)

Half-eagle and half-lion, the griffin was a majestic, mythological Greek creature. It was said to guard treasure and even lay golden eggs.

Many ancient cultures, like the Greeks, Egyptians, and Persians, considered me sacred. They all agreed I was the king of beasts!

It had the wings of an eagle.

Tail of a lion

Pegasus

Pegasus was the magical, winged horse from Greek mythology. It sprang from the neck of the monster, Medusa (*meh–DOO–sah*), after the hero Perseus (*PER–see–uss*) cut off her head.

Pegasus was shown as a beautiful white horse with large wings.

I had many adventures with the hero Bellerophon (*bel-ler-o-phon*) but threw him off when he tried to ride me to Mount Olympus, home of the gods.

Super facts

Pronunciation: peh-guh-suhs
Origin: Greek mythology **Location:** Greece and western coast of Türkiye (Turkey) **Characteristics:** Huge wings, incredible speed, superstrength, noble
Lookalike: Devadatta (Hindu)

Minokawa

Minokawa was a giant, dragon-like bird in Filipino folklore. It was said to be so big that it could swallow the Sun, Moon, and Earth.

Sharp, sword-like feathers

Its legs and claws were sometimes shown to be made of steel.

In ancient times, people believed that I caused an eclipse of the Sun by swallowing it whole.

Super facts

Pronunciation: mee-noh-KAH-wah   **Origin:** Filipino folklore
Location: Philippines   **Characteristics:** Enormous size, superstrength, steel claws, associated with eclipses   **Lookalikes:** Fenghuang (Chinese), Garuda (Hindu), roc (Persian)

Sarimanok

The Maranao people believed that their crops would grow large if they worshipped me.

Sarimanok was a mythical bird worshipped by the Maranao people of the Philippines. Thought to be a link between the seen and unseen worlds, it remains a popular symbol today.

Sarimanok was depicted as a type of rooster with bright, colourful feathers.

Super facts

Pronunciation: sah-ree-mah-nok   **Origin:** Filipino folklore
Location: Philippines   **Characteristics:** Vibrant plumage, symbol of prosperity, protector, messenger, associated with royalty   **Lookalikes:** Firebird (Russian), Garuda (Hindu), phoenix (Greek)

Dragons

From slithering Greek serpents to winged English wyverns, mythology has many dragons. However, not all of them flew, breathed fire, or fought knights in armour. The dragons of China and Korea were kind and brought good luck.

 Large, pointed horns

Kur

The Kur (*koor*) was a monstrous ancient Sumerian dragon who kidnapped the goddess of the underworld and then became its ruler. He was killed by the gods Enki and Ninurta.

Basilisk

The Basilisk (*BAS-ih-lisk*) was a terrifying European dragon that could kill simply with its stare. With the body of a snake and the head of a cockerel, the basilisk had to avoid mirrors, or it would die of fright.

Imugi

The imugi (*ee-MOO-gee*) was a kind, snake-like Korean creature that lived in water and dark caves. After 1,000 years, an imugi could grow into a fully fledged, adult dragon.

Kuh Billaur

The Persian dragon Kuh Billaur
(*koo-BILL-owr*) had sharp fangs and a
long, muscular body, like a python.
It famously fought the legendary hero
Ali, who slayed it with his sword.

Kuh Billaur had a scaly,
snake-like body.

Tianlóng

In China, dragons are called lóngs, and Tianlóng
(*tee-AHN-long*) was a celestial dragon that
guarded the stars. Believed to bring good
luck, these mythical creatures took their
power from a magical pearl.

Ryū depicted alongside
a woman playing a koto, a
Japanese musical instrument.

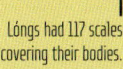

Lóngs had 117 scales
covering their bodies.

Ryū

The Japanese Ryū (*ree-yoo*) was a wingless,
serpent-like dragon, with a body covered
in scales and a long, pointed tail. Ryū
was a symbol of wisdom, power,
and good fortune.

Totem poles

Totem poles are sacred monuments created by the Indigenous peoples of the Pacific Northwest region. Typically carved from cedar trees, totem poles show creatures and beings, and also represent history, ancestry, peoples, or events.

Thunderbird

Many Indigenous peoples of the Pacific Northwest worshipped a powerful spirit called the Thunderbird. Taking the form of a bird of prey, it was believed to bring precious rains, cause lightning, and make thunderclaps by beating its wings.

Super facts

Pronunciation: THUN-der-bird
Origin: Mythology of Indigenous peoples of the Pacific Northwest **Location:** North America, Africa, Asia, and Europe
Characteristics: Three pairs of powerful wings, lighting bolts under the largest pair, plumage on head **Lookalikes:** Garuda (Hindu), griffin (Greek), roc (Middle Eastern), Simurgh (Persian)

Did you know?
Some people believed the Thunderbird could grant humans powerful skills and supernatural abilities.

Bright feathers

Was believed to flash lightning from its beak

It is said that the Thunderbird protected humans against harmful sea creatures. In one story, the Thunderbird saves the people from starvation by killing a whale that frightened away all the salmon.

Simurgh

In Persian mythology, Simurgh (*see-merg*) is a magical bird that flies between Earth and the heavens. She is said to be strong enough to fly for long distances carrying elephants and whales. Stories about Simurgh are very old – she is believed to have seen the world being destroyed and reborn three times over.

Sphinx

With the legs of a lion, the wings of an eagle, and the head of a woman, the Sphinx (*SFINX*) was a terrifying creature to behold. She was also smart, merciless, and hungry for human flesh.

The Sphinx was often shown sitting while she posed her riddles.

The Greek Sphinx was probably based on similar creatures from Mesopotamia and Egypt.

Sphinx: Merciless, mind-bending monster

Battle up!

The son of King Laius, Oedipus was fated to kill his father. To avoid this prophecy, he went searching for answers in Thebes (an ancient Egyptian city). But his path was blocked by a monster called Sphinx.

Oedipus

Before he came across the Sphinx, Oedipus [*EE-di-puss*] had already killed a chariot driver on the road. The Sphinx was asking passers-by a riddle and then devouring those who could not answer. Oedipus decided to enter this battle of the minds.

Oedipus was usually depicted in his travelling clothes, consisting of a cape, toga, and sandals.

After learning of the prophecy, Oedipus's parents abandoned him. He was raised by the Corinthian king Polybus.

Oedipus: Wise-witted, mind-battling warrior

Who wins?

The Sphinx asked Oedipus a riddle and got ready to devour him, but Oedipus answered the riddle correctly. The Sphinx died of shame. Now a hero, Oedipus married the Queen of Thebes. Later, he found out that the chariot driver he had killed in a fit of rage was King Laius. The prophecy had come true!

Winner!

Firebird

According to Slavic folklore, the firebird was a magical, golden-feathered creature that could bring either blessings or misfortune to anyone who caught it. The firebird often featured in fairy tales with kings, heroes, and princesses.

Just one feather from the firebird's tail was said to be enough to light an entire dark room.

The king ordered the archer to catch the firebird as it had been stealing golden apples from the king's orchard.

In a famous fairy tale, an archer found a firebird's feather and gave it to his king. But the king then demanded the whole firebird, followed by a series of ever more difficult tasks. In the end, the archer's fortune turned and he became the king.

When the firebird sang, pearls were said to fall from its eyes.

Did you know?
Like the firebird, the phoenix is a magical bird from Greek mythology. It burns in its own fire after living for hundreds of years, then rises from its ashes.

Super facts

Pronunciation: FIRE-bird
Origin: Slavic folklore   **Location:** Slavic countries
Characteristics: Golden feathers, eyes like crystal, majestic plumage that glows brightly
Lookalikes: Bennu (Egyptian), fenghuang (Chinese), Garuda (Hindu), Huma (Persian), phoenix (Greek)

Jatayu

In Hindu mythology, Jatayu was a huge, divine bird and king of vultures. He tried to rescue Sita (wife of the deity Rama) from the demon king Ravana, who chopped off his wings.

As I lay dying, I told Rama his wife was kidnapped and pointed him in the direction she was taken.

Jatayu was a large vulture with a massive wingspan.

Super facts

Pronunciation: juh-taa-yoo
Origin: Hindu mythology
Location: South Asia   **Characteristic:** Demigod in the form of a vulture
Lookalikes: Nekhbet (Egyptian), Sampati (Hindu)

Garuda

Part–man and part–eagle, Garuda was a Hindu demigod. He devoured evil people and carried the god Vishnu on his daily journey across the sky.

Super facts

Pronunciation: ga-ROO-dah
Origin: Hindu mythology
Location: South Asia
Characteristics: Emerald-coloured eyes, golden wings, legs like those of a kite bird
Lookalikes: Kalavinka (Buddhist), karura (Japanese), siren (Greek)

Golden wings of an eagle

Arms and upper body of a man

It is said that I hatched from a giant egg at the beginning of time and later became immortal.

Gamayun

With the body of a bird and the head of a woman, the Gamayun was a mythical messenger from Russian folklore. She was said to know the fate of every god, hero, and mortal in the Universe.

In the Slavir folklore of Eastern Europe, the Alkonost [al-koh-nost] was a bird with a woman's head similar to the Gamayun. It was said that anyone who heard the Alkonost sing would forget everything they knew.

Super facts

Pronunciation: ga-ma-yun
Origin: Russian folklore
Location: Slavic countries
Characteristics: Half-bird and half-woman, enchanting voice
Lookalikes: Anzu (Sumerian), Garuda (Hindu), lamassu (Mesopotamian), siren (Greek)

The bright, divine depiction of the bird represented peace and harmony.

Did you know?
Gamayun's hymns were magical but her voice was difficult to understand. Those who were able to make sense of her words were gifted good fortune.

Bennu

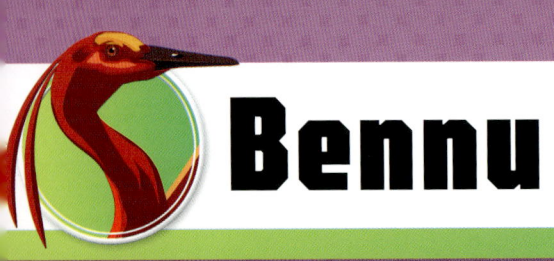

An Egyptian deity that took the form of a heron, Bennu was connected with the Sun, creation, and rebirth. Its cry brought an end to silence in the Universe and began the creation of the world.

I am the inspiration for the phoenix – a mythological bird that rose from the ashes to be reborn.

Ba

In ancient Egyptian mythology, Ba was the part of a person's spirit that came into being after death. Ba usually appeared as a falcon, with the head of a human.

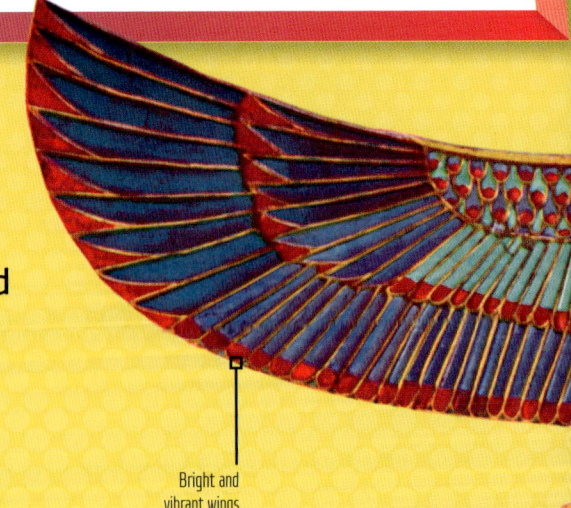

Bright and vibrant wings

Bennu's fiery, colourful feathers represented the flames of creation.

Super facts

Pronunciation: BEN-oo
Origin: Egyptian mythology
Location: Egypt and northeastern Africa
Characteristics: Long beak, two-feathered crest
Lookalikes: Firebird (Russian), phoenix (Greek)

Ba's human head was depicted wearing a traditional Egyptian headdress.

People carried statues of me during funeral services for the dead.

Super facts

Pronunciation: BAR
Origin: Egyptian mythology
Location: Egypt and northeastern Africa
Characteristics: Body and wings of a falcon, head of a human
Lookalikes: Alkonost and Gamayun (Slavic), Garuda (Hindu)

Hamsa bird

In Hindu mythology, the Hamsa (*hum-sa)* was a sacred bird that looked like a swan or goose. It was considered to be a symbol of purity and knowledge. It is believed that the god Brahma and Saraswati (*sa–ras–vat–ee*), the goddess of knowledge and learning, often rode the Hamsa.

Legends of the water

Sink beneath the waves to find great mythological monsters of the deep. Here dwell dastardly creatures, such as the ship-crushing Kraken, the child-stealing qallupilluit, and the sailor-swallowing Charybdis. But there are kinder water legends, too. Seal-skinned selkies often help humans, while mermaids sometimes guide shipwrecked seafarers to shore.

Qallupilluit

Qallupilluit were coastal, child–snatching monsters from Inuit mythology. They lived in the Arctic Ocean, often under sea ice, waiting for young victims to stray too close to the water. Then, they would strike!

> I leap from the sea to grab children by the shore, then stash them in my duck-skin pouch and swim to the bottom.

Scaly skin and claw-like fingernails

Super facts

Pronunciation: qalloo-pilloo-it   **Origin:** Inuit mythology
Location: Arctic and subarctic   **Characteristics:** Slimy skin, long hair and fingernails   **Lookalikes:** Grindylow (English), nuckelavee (Scottish), typhon (Greek), wendigo (North American)

Yacumama

A monster of South American folklore, the Yacumama was a massive serpent that lived in the Amazon Rainforest. Lying in wait in rivers, it would ambush any animal within its grasp.

Super facts

Pronunciation: ya-koo-ma-ma
Origin: South American mythology
Location: Peru, Brazil, Colombia, Ecuador, and Bolivia **Characteristics:** Huge body, long and sharp teeth
Lookalikes: Jörmungandr (Norse), Tiamat (Babylonian)

The Yacumama was said to be more than 60 m (197 ft) long.

My name means "Mother of the Waters" and I am known as the greatest of all sea creatures.

Kraken

The Kraken was the legendary terror of the seas. This tentacled monster rose from the deep to drag entire ships below the surface. Sailors reported the creature looked like a cross between a squid and an octopus; some said it grew to the size of an island.

Super facts

Pronunciation: kra-ken
Origin: Norse mythology
Location: North Atlantic and northern Europe
Characteristics: Squiggly arms covered in suckers, beak-like mouth
Lookalikes: Akkorokamui (Japanese), hafgufa (Icelandic), lusca (Caribbean), te wheke-a-muturangi (Māori)

People have claimed to spot the Kraken for thousands of years, although no one has ever caught the creature. It famously inspired the monster in Jules Verne's novel, *Twenty Thousand Leagues Under the Sea*.

The Kraken's tentacles were said to be long enough to wrap around a ship's mast.

Did you know?
In 1734, Scandinavian bishop Hans Egede reported the Kraken's body was four times longer than his ship and its head higher than the mast.

Eyes as big as dinner plates

Hippocampus

Super facts

Pronunciation: hi-PO-KAM-puss
Origin: Greek mythology
Location: Greece and western coast of Türkiye (Turkey)
Characteristics: Half-horse, half-fish, lucky omen   **Lookalike:** Kelpie (Scottish)

Hippocampus had the body of a horse and the tail of a fish. This Greek sea creature was known to pull the chariot of Poseidon, the Greek god of the sea.

I was often depicted in temples, wall paintings, and coins in ancient Greece and Rome.

With the tail of a fish, the hippocampus was a good swimmer.

Loch Ness monster

The Loch Ness monster is a mythological marine creature said to live in Scotland's Loch Ness. People have reported seeing the monster for more than 1,400 years, but its existence is yet to be proven.

Super facts

Pronunciation: lok-NESS monster
Origin: Scottish folklore
Location: Scotland
Characteristics: Multi-humped, dark, scaly, and serpent-like body
Lookalikes: Leviathan (Jewish), Hydra (Greek)

Were often depicted as the prehistoric reptile Plesiosaurus, with long neck and flippers to swim through water

Some people believe that I rose to the surface and bit a man in 565 CE, but there is no proof that it actually happened.

Sea serpents

Shaped like massive, monstrous snakes, sea serpents were the underwater terrors of myths and legends. Many of these creatures dwelled deep below the ocean waves, and only rose up to sink ships and swallow sailors whole.

Shesha was usually depicted with multiple heads.

Shesha

Shesha [*shay-shah*], also called Ananta, was a creator serpent and the king of the nagas from Hindu mythology. In most depictions, Vishnu can be seen resting on this multiheaded serpent, while it floated in the cosmic ocean.

Jörmungandr's mouth was big enough to swallow a god whole.

Jörmungandr

Also known as the Midgard Serpent, Jörmungandr [*YOR-mun-gan-der*] was an enormous, evil serpent of Norse mythology. It encircled the world of humans with its body and bit down on its own tail.

Leviathan

Leviathan [*luh-vai-uh-thn*] was a Biblical beast that had many heads and lived in the deepest ocean. It wanted to unleash chaos upon the world, but was defeated by the angel Gabriel who used its skin as a tent.

Taniwha

In Māori mythology, taniwha [*ta-nee-wah*] were supernatural, shapeshifting creatures that took the form of sea serpents, lizards, and sharks. Some taniwha would kill, kidnap, and eat people. Others were worshipped as the guardians of a particular tribe.

Had a thick, finned mane

Inkanyamba

The Inkanyamba [*in-can-yam-ba*] was a snake-like creature with the head of a horse. This monster from Zulu mythology was known to live in South Africa's Howick Falls. It was believed to be responsible for destructive, summertime storms.

Scylla

A supernatural sea monster, Scylla guarded one side of the Strait of Messina, between Italy and Sicily. It was said to devour every sailor that passed within reach.

I used to be a beautiful sea nymph until the goddess Circe turned me into a vengeful monster.

Had six heads on long, snake-like necks

Super facts

Pronunciation: SILL-a   **Origin:** Greek mythology
Location: Greece and western coast of Türkiye (Turkey)
Characteristics: Six snake heads, human torso, superstrength
Lookalikes: Hydra (Greek), naga (Hindu)

Charybdis

Charybdis was a gigantic sea monster that lived on the other side of the Strait of Messina, opposite to Scylla. It took the form of a great whirlpool that could suck down entire ships and smash them into pieces.

Super facts

Pronunciation: ka-RIB-diss
Origin: Greek mythology
Location: Greece and western coast of Türkiye (Turkey)
Characteristics: Huge mouth, giant whirlpool, rows of sharp teeth
Lookalike: Kraken (Norse)

The terrifying choice between facing me or Scylla led to a saying "between Scylla and Charybdis" meaning "between two equally bad situations".

Sharp teeth

Gaping mouth

Mermaid

Mermaids were mythical marine creatures with the head and torso of a human, and the tail of a fish. Mermaids lived at sea, but could befriend and even marry humans on land.

Did you know?
Mermaids could be both helpful and harmful. Kind mermaids would help shipwreck victims, whereas others would drown sailors by luring them into the sea.

Mermaids could be vain and often kept a mirror close by.

Super facts

Pronunciation: merr-maid
Origin: Mesopotamian mythology
Location: Middle East
Characteristics: Woman with the tail of a fish, hypnotic voice, enchanting beauty
Lookalikes: Gulnare of the Sea (Persian), Jiāo rén (Chinese), Undine (European)

Triton (*try-ton*), the Greek demigod of the sea, was a male mermaid, or merman. He had the top half of a man and the bottom half of a fish, and lived in a golden palace at the bottom of the sea.

Kappa

Super facts

Pronunciation: KAP-pah
Origin: Japanese folklore
Location: East Asia
Characteristics: Green skin, turtle-like shell, monkey-like face with a beak
Lookalikes: Grindylow (English), kelpie (Scottish), yōkai (Japanese)

Kappa were Japanese turtle–like demon with a monkey face. They lured people into the rivers and ponds where they lived. The kappa would then drown their victims and feed on them.

We love cucumbers! If a person inscribes their name on a cucumber and throws it into our waters, we will not harm them.

Were usually shown with green skin, and webbed hands and feet

Umibōzu

Some people say that we are the spirits of priests drowned by bloodthirsty villagers.

The Umibōzu was a mysterious marine monster that took the shape of a giant human. It would rise up from its deep–sea lair to smash up ships and drown their crews.

Super facts

Pronunciation: oo-me-boh-zoo
Origin: Japanese folklore
Location: East Asia
Characteristics: Incredibly tall, shaved head, entirely black
Lookalikes: Adaro (Melanesian), Kraken (Slavic)

Umibōzu were said to have inky black skin.

Ninki Nanka

In the folklore of Gambia, Ninki Nanka was an evil, dragon-like creature that lurked in swamps and preyed on people. It could paralyse its prey with a look, before eating them alive.

Super facts

Pronunciation: NIN-kee NAN-kah
Origin: Gambian folklore
Location: West Africa
Characteristics: Shapeshifting, reflective scales, head crest
Lookalike: Loch Ness Monster (Scottish)

Horse-like head

Giraffe's neck

Body of a crocodile

I can take many forms to lure victims into the swamp. The best way to defeat me is with a mirror, which stops me in my tracks!

Jengu

The jengu was a mermaid–like water spirit. It lived in the oceans, rivers, and lakes, and could bring good luck to those who made offerings to it.

As a guardian spirit, I control the fate of all humans and animals that enter Earth's waterways.

Jengu was usually depicted as a beautiful mermaid with long hair.

Super facts

Pronunciation: jen-guh
Origin: Cameroon folklore
Location: Central and West Africa
Characteristics: Gappy teeth, mermaid-like, long hair
Lookalikes: Jiaoren (Chinese), undine (Europe)

Underwater worlds

Stories of sunken cities and civilizations submerged by the sea have fascinated people for centuries. Some stories speak of lost worlds that exist only in mythologies. Others are about real places that lie hidden beneath the waves.

This statue of the Nile god Hapi, made between 664 and 120 BCE, was recovered from the ruins of Thonis-Heracleion.

Atlantis

The legendary island Atlantis lay somewhere in the Atlantic Ocean. Ruled by the rich Atlantians, the island was supposedly struck by earthquakes and swallowed by the sea.

Thonis-Heracleion

Founded around 2,700 years ago, the Egyptian city of Thonis-Heracleion was built on islands at the end of the River Nile. However, the city sunk after a series of storms and has only been recently rediscovered.

Dwarka

According to Hindu mythology, Dwarka was an ancient city founded by the god Krishna as his capital. It was said to have sunk beneath the Arabian Sea after Krishna left Earth to join the spiritual world.

This map shows the lost continent where Kásskara (the Hopi name for Lemuria) would have possibly been.

Kásskara

In the folklore of the North American Hopi peoples, Kásskara was their original homeland. An Atlantic island the size of a continent, Kásskara eventually sank, leaving only the remnants of Hawaii behind.

Kitezh

Kitezh was a mythical Russian city supposedly built on the shores of Lake Svetloyar in the 13th century. In the legend, the city burst into countless fountains and sank after Mongol invaders appeared at its gates.

Artwork showing the migration from Aztlan

Mysterious island

The homeland of the Aztecs, Aztlan was a city built on an island lake somewhere in northwestern Mexico. This map shows the Aztecs migrating from Aztlan to their new home of Tenochtitlan. Today, the existence of Aztlan remains a mystery.

Apotamkin

A sea monster, Apotamkin lived in North America's Passamaquoddy Bay. It preyed on people walking along the shore and pulled them into the water to feed on them.

Adults often shared stories of me to teach children the importance of listening to their parents.

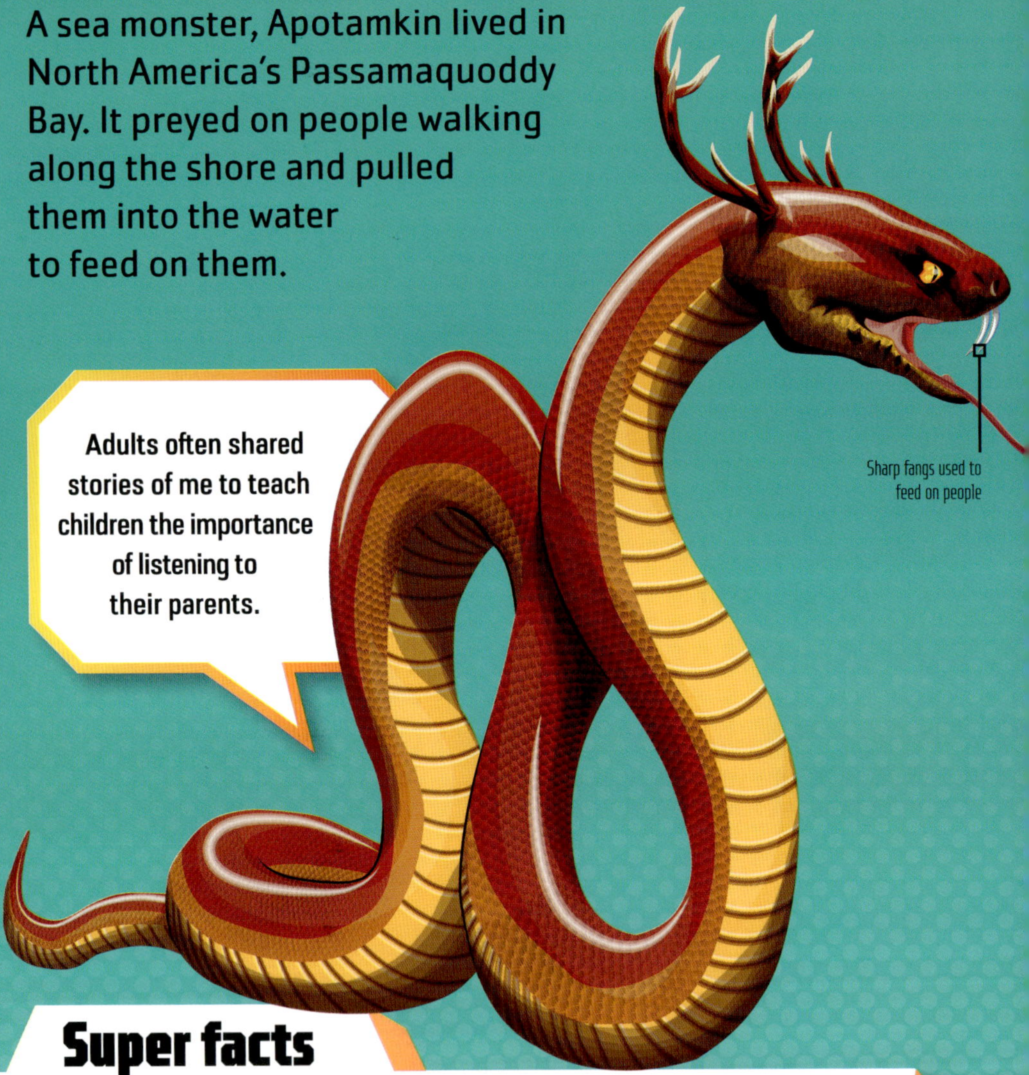

Sharp fangs used to feed on people

Super facts

Pronunciation: uh-POH-tam-kin
Origin: Folklore of Indigenous peoples of the Pacific Northwest   **Location:** North America
Characteristics: Aquatic monster, predator, control over water and storms, shapeshifter

Mishipeshu

Also called the Underwater Panther, Mishipeshu was a dangerous aquatic monster that lived in lakes. It caused whirlpools, violent waves, and storms to strike humans on the water's surface and drown them.

> Many people believe I dwell in Lake Superior and am known as its protector.

Thought to have the head of a cat

Super facts

Pronunciation: mee-shee-peh-shooh   **Origin:** Folklore of Indigenous peoples of the Pacific Northwest   **Location:** North America   **Characteristics:** Scaly body, spiny back, control over water and storms

165

Selkie

Selkies were shapeshifting mythical creatures that lived in water as seals. When on land, they were said to shed their skin and become humans. Sometimes selkies were friendly and helpful, but at other times they could be dangerous and harmful.

Super facts

Pronunciation: SEL-kee
Origin: Scottish, Celtic, and Norse folklores   **Location:** Northwestern Europe
Characteristics: Half-seal, half-human
Lookalikes: Gulnare of the sea (Persian), Jiaoren (Chinese), mermaid (Mesopotamian), siren (Greek), Undine (European)

I am a female selkie who married a fisherman. He hid my seal skin to prevent me from leaving him. But when I found it, I returned back to the sea forever.

Usually depicted in their seal form in the water or on the beach

Bunyip

Adults usually told children stories about me to warn them to stay away from water holes.

In First Australian folklore, the Bunyip was a legendary monster that lived in swamps. It was said to make an ear–shattering roar. The Bunyip devoured humans, especially women and children.

Sharp fangs

Super facts

Pronunciation: BUN-yip
Origin: First Australian folklore
Location: South East Australia
Characteristics: Body resembling that of an ox, hippopotamus, or manatee
Lookalikes: Näkki (Finnish), kappa (Japanese)

167

Cipactli

A sea monster from Aztec mythology, Cipactli was sometimes depicted as part–crocodile, part–toad, and part–fish. It was said to have multiple mouths all over its body and was always hungry for a new victim.

The gods regretted creating me after I started eating every creature in sight! They then set out to catch and destroy me.

Elongated body, covered in thick, tough scales

Super facts

Pronunciation: see-PAK-tlee   **Origin:** Aztec mythology
Location: Central and southern Mexico
Characteristics: Always hungry, has features of crocodiles, fish, toads, and frogs, every joint has a mouth
Lookalikes: Makara (Hindu), Sobek (Egyptian)

Ahuizotl

The Aztec Ahuizotl was a small, aquatic monster that killed people who wandered into the water. It was said to live in the lakes and rivers of Tenochtitlan (*ten–nosh–ti–clan*), the Aztec capital.

Super facts

Pronunciation: ah-wee-SOH-tl
Origin: Aztec mythology
Location: Central and southern Mexico
Characteristics: Waterproof fur, dark coloured, sharp teeth
Lookalikes: Púca (Celtic), puma (Inca)

Long tail with a sharp claw

When in water, all Aztecs feared me. I would use my fangs to pull out their eyes, teeth, and nails!

Kiwa

Super facts

Pronunciation: kee-wah
Origin: Māori mythology
Location: Polynesian islands
Characteristic: Guardian who controlled the ocean
Lookalike: Oceanus (Greek)

In Māori mythology, Kiwa was a guardian of the ocean. He travelled from Hawaiki, the ancestral land, to discover parts of the east coast on the island of Te Ika-a-Māui in modern-day New Zealand.

I sailed to Aotearoa (the Māori name for New Zealand) aboard the legendary *Tākitimu* canoe.

Kiwa was depicted as a powerful Māori warrior.

Usually shown rising over powerful ocean waves

Dakuwaqa

A sea monster and shark deity from Fijian mythology, Dakuwaqa acted as a guardian of the ocean. He was a favourite among fishermen, who believed he would protect them at sea.

> I once battled an enormous octopus, which pulled out all of my teeth! But I still won.

Depicted as a strong, muscular man with the features of a shark

Super facts

Pronunciation: da-koo-wah-ka
Origin: Fijian mythology
Location: Oceania
Characteristics: Sea guardian, body of a man and features of a shark
Lookalikes: Makara (Hindu), Triton (Greek)

171

Ushi-Oni

A terrifying creature from Japanese folklore, the Ushi-Oni (*OO-shee-o-nee*) was believed to have the head of an ox, a spider's body, sharp fangs, and a thin, darting tongue. It had a taste for human flesh and would prowl coastal regions in search of prey. To kill its victims, the Ushi-Oni would spit poison at them before feasting on their bodies.

Mythical creatures

Mythical creatures come in all shapes and sizes and many are a combination of several different animals. Some are grotesque and terrifying, such as the multiheaded monster Cerberus, while others are magnificent and noble, like the flying horse Pegasus. Regardless of whether they are good or bad, each creature has a role to play.

Centaur

Half–horse and half–man, centaurs were wild, savage, and lawless creatures. They dwelled in the mountains of Thessaly, Greece, and were good fighters.

Centaurs were skilled at using many weapons including the bow and arrow.

There are carvings of us in the square panels of the Parthenon temple in Greece.

Super facts

Pronunciation: SEN-tor
Origin: Greek mythology **Location:** Greece and western coast of Türkiye (Turkey) **Characteristics:** Superstrength, body of a horse, torso and head of a man
Lookalikes: Faun (Greek), satyr (Greek)

Satyr

With the legs of a goat and the upper body of a man, satyrs were crafty forest spirits. They lived to drink wine, chase nymphs, and play tricks on people.

Super facts

Pronunciation: SA-teer
Origin: Greek mythology
Location: Greece and western coast of Türkiye (Turkey)
Characteristics: Half-goat, half-man
Lookalikes: Centaur (Greek), faun (Greek)

All us satyrs were the followers of Dionysus (*dai-oh-NAI-suss*), the Greek god of wine.

Satyrs had the legs and tail of a goat.

Werewolf

According to folklore, a werewolf was a human that turned into a wolf, usually during the night of the full Moon. It would hunt and devour people and animals at night, and at daybreak return to its human form.

Super facts

Pronunciation: wer-wulf
Origin: Greek mythology   **Location:** Greece and western coast of Türkiye (Turkey)
Characteristics: Human that transforms into a wolf, superstrength, superhuman senses
Lookalikes: Buda (Ethiopian), Erchitu (Sardinian), ichchhadhari naga (Hindu)

In Greek mythology, the cruel king Lycaon tried to trick Zeus, the king of the gods, into eating human flesh. As punishment, Zeus unleashed a great flood and turned Lycaon into a wolf. This story is one of the earliest examples of werewolves in mythology where a human transforms into a wolf.

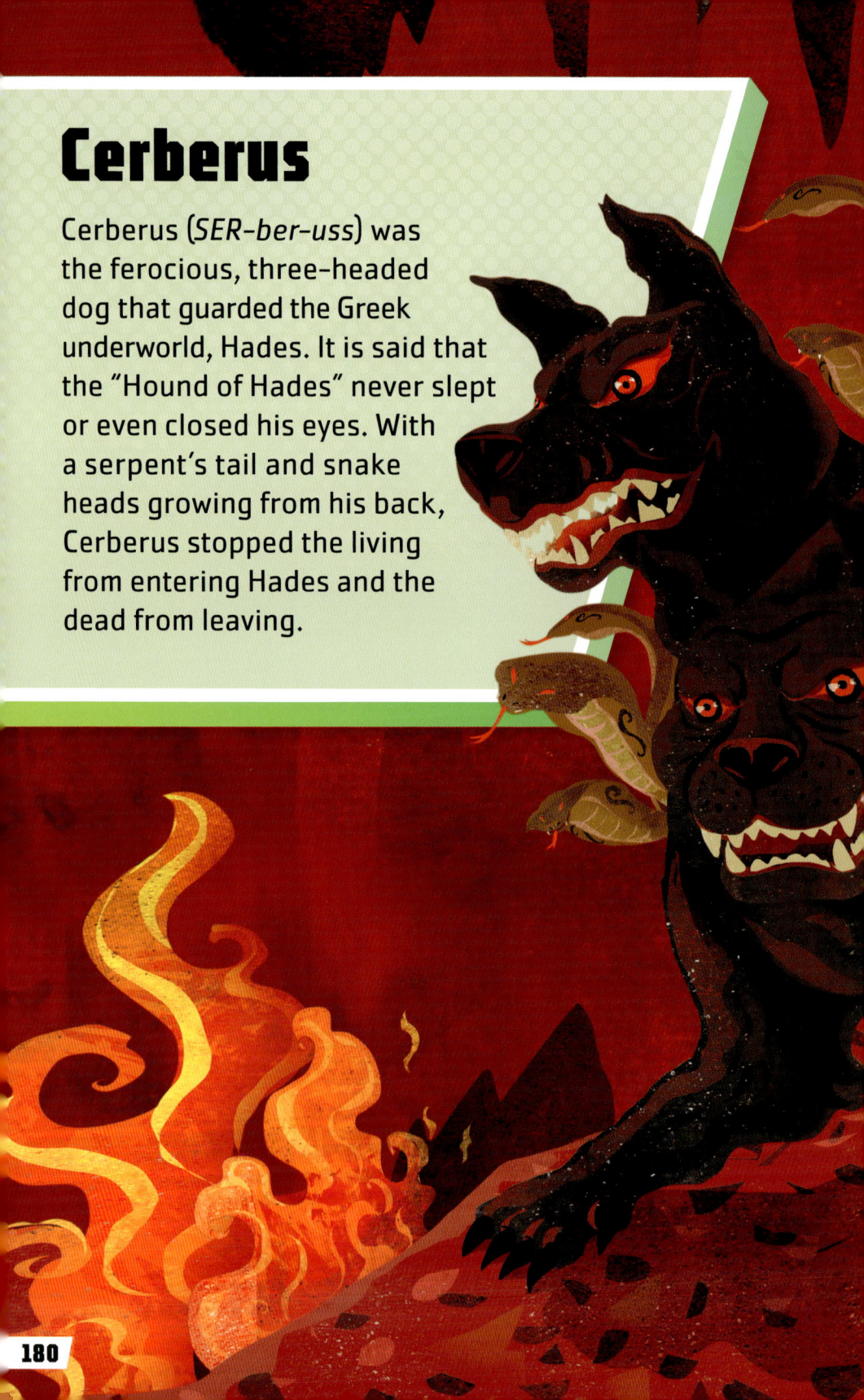

Cerberus

Cerberus (*SER-ber-uss*) was
the ferocious, three-headed
dog that guarded the Greek
underworld, Hades. It is said that
the "Hound of Hades" never slept
or even closed his eyes. With
a serpent's tail and snake
heads growing from his back,
Cerberus stopped the living
from entering Hades and the
dead from leaving.

Theseus

To save the Athenians from the terrifying Minotaur, the brave prince of Athens, Theseus (*THEE-see-uss*), volunteered to be one of the offerings sent to King Minos. He was determined to defeat the monster and free his people.

Minos's daughter gave Theseus a sword to defend himself.

Ariadne, Minos's daughter, gave Theseus a ball of thread to find his way in and out of the labyrinth.

Theseus: Mighty slayer of evil creatures

Battle up!

Crete and Athens had battled for years until the Athenians surrendered. King Minos of Crete then demanded that each year, seven boys and seven girls from Athens be sent as offerings to his half-man, half-bull monster, the Minotaur.

Minotaur

With the body of a human and the head of a bull, the Minotaur (*MAI-noh-tor*) was the son of Pasiphae, Minos's wife. Due to his uncontrollable power and relentless hunger for humans and animals, he was confined within a labyrinth that was nearly impossible to escape.

Bull-like tail

The Minotaur was originally named Asterion, meaning "the starry one".

Minotaur: Invincible bull-headed beast

Who wins?

Blessed by the gods, Theseus embarked on his quest to defeat the Minotaur, guided by a carefully laid thread to find his way in the labyrinth. After a fierce battle, he dealt a fatal blow by plunging his sword beneath the Minotaur's arm, bringing the beast down. Wounded but victorious, Theseus staggered out of the maze.

Winner!

Troll

The original trolls from Norse folklore were giants who lived in castles and turned to stone if struck by sunlight. Later, trolls were described as small and ugly creatures that lived in caves, forests, and under bridges.

Trolls were said to have thick, rough skin.

I steal human babies and take them to my mountain, where I devour them.

Super facts

Pronunciation: TROL
Origin: Norse folklore
Location: North Atlantic and northern Europe
Characteristics: Huge eyes, big nose, large ears
Lookalike: Dokkaebi (Korean)

Dwarf

In Norse mythology, dwarfs were small men with long beards, who lived underground and made precious objects for the gods. They were particularly skilled at forging magical weapons and attractive jewellery.

Super facts

Pronunciation: DWORF
Origin: Norse mythology
Location: North Atlantic and northern Europe **Characteristics:** Superstrength, short and bushy hair
Lookalike: Leprechaun (Irish)

I am a mountain dwarf. We live in tribes, with our own kings, chiefs, and armies.

Short and heavily-built

Hel

The Norse goddess of the underworld, Hel was a terrifying figure. Half of her body was alive and the other half was a rotting corpse. She ruled over dead people who had perished from old age or disease.

My siblings are Fenrir and Jörmungandr, and we are all children of the trickster god, Loki.

In some depictions, Hel was shown with a staff.

The rotting half of her body often showed the skeleton below.

Super facts

Pronunciation: hell
Origin: Norse mythology
Location: North Atlantic and northern Europe
Characteristics: Half-dead and half-alive   **Lookalikes:** Hades (Greek), Yama (Hindu)

Fenrir

Fenrir was the giant wolf that helped destroy the Norse universe and devoured Odin, the king of the gods. He had a gaping mouth full of fangs, and fire burned from his eyes and nostrils.

Super facts

Pronunciation: FEN-reer
Origin: Norse mythology
Location: North Atlantic and northern Europe
Characteristics: Superstrength, huge size
Lookalikes: Amarok (Inuit), Lupa (Roman)

The Norse dwarfs had to make the strongest chain in the world to hold Fenrir.

I was once the pet of the Asgard gods, but they chained me up after I grew large and dangerous.

Insulæ Fortunatæ

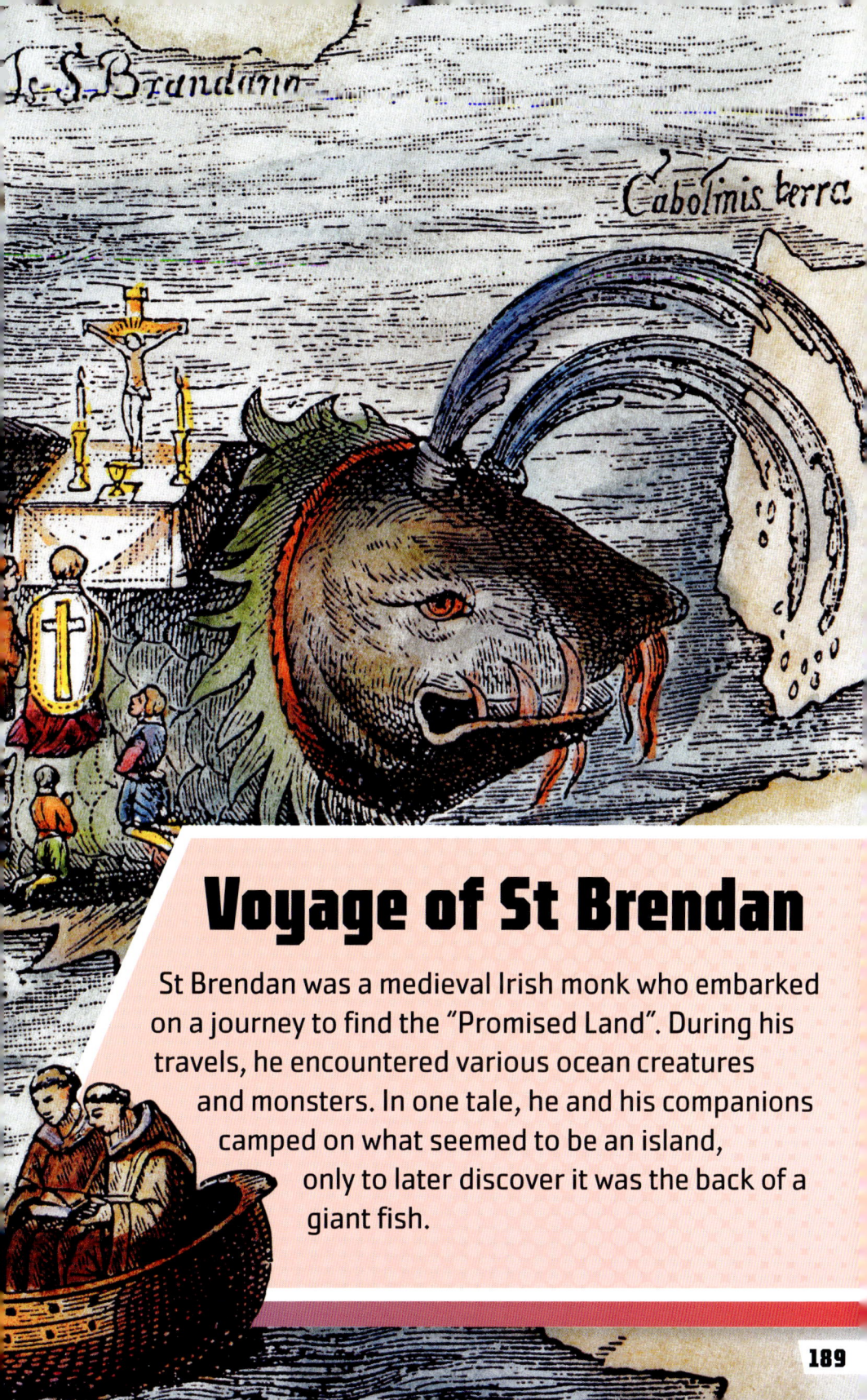

Is S. Brandann

Cabolinis terra

Voyage of St Brendan

St Brendan was a medieval Irish monk who embarked on a journey to find the "Promised Land". During his travels, he encountered various ocean creatures and monsters. In one tale, he and his companions camped on what seemed to be an island, only to later discover it was the back of a giant fish.

Mischief-makers

Mythology is full of spirits and magical creatures who caused trouble wherever they went. Even today, people blame these miniature mischief–makers for blunt knives, sour milk, or scary sounds in forests.

Did you know?

The first gnomes were said to live underground guarding treasure. Today, gnome statues are often found in private gardens and public parks.

Gnomes

Originally spirits that could move through the Earth, gnomes [*NOME*] became small, mischief-making men in later European folklore. They were most commonly believed to cause household chaos, such as making people oversleep.

Bake-danuki

In Japanese folklore, bake-danuki (*ba-kay-dan-oo-kee*) were strange, supernatural shapeshifters that usually looked like racoon dogs. The bake-danuki were best known for committing acts of mischief, such as turning into loud drums to scare people travelling through the woods.

Were often shown dressed in green, but they were originally said to wear red

Elves

In Norse mythology, elves (*elvz*) were formed from maggots and were either light (good), or dark (evil). Later, fairy-tale elves could be helpful, make mischief, or cause harm. Some fixed shoes and made sculptures, while others brought bad dreams, and some even stole children.

Leprechauns

In Irish folklore, leprechauns (*lep-ruh-kawns*) were tiny, bearded men who lived in remote places, made shoes, and brought mischief to passers-by. In fairy tales, leprechauns stashed away pots of gold, but usually tricked people who wanted to find it.

Unicorn

The unicorn was a mythical beast with the body of a white horse and a single, spiral–shaped horn on its head. It was believed that drinking from a unicorn's horn could provide protection against poison.

Super facts

Pronunciation: YOO-ni-korn
Origin: Hindu and Chinese mythology
Location: South and East Asia
Characteristics: Graceful, elusive, superspeed, very wise, healer
Lookalikes: Chollima (Korean), Sleipnir (Norse), qílín (Chinese)

During the excavation of the ancient city of Mohenjo-daro, present-day Pakistan, a wax seal was uncovered with a unicorn motif. It was roughly dated back to 2000 BCE.

The unicorn's sharp horn was believed to have magical qualities.

Did you know?
Cups made of unicorn horns were highly prized in Medieval Europe. However, they were probably made from the tusks of a narwhal.

Colourful mane

Was sometimes depicted with cloven hooves

Blud

Blud was an evil Slavic spirit that cast spells to confuse people and make them wander aimlessly for days. Sometimes Blud led its victims through dangerous forests, into swamps, or off cliffs.

Blud carried a special wooden staff to cast spells with.

I often make people walk around in small circles, for my entertainment.

Was sometimes shown as a long-bearded, forest dweller

Super facts

Pronunciation: BLUD
Origin: Slavic mythology
Location: Eastern and Central Europe, and parts of Asia
Characteristics: Trickster, cause of chaos, evil fairy
Lookalike: Will-o'-the-wisp (English)

Polevik

A Russian field spirit that appeared at noon, the Polevik was both helpful and harmful. It helped harvest crops, but also led travellers astray, sometimes strangling unaware people to death.

I like to ride horses at breakneck speed and run down anyone that gets in the way!

Super facts

Pronunciation: poh-leh-veek
Origin: Russian folklore
Location: Slavic countries
Characteristics: Head covered with green grass, height grows and shrinks with the crops
Lookalikes: Leshy (Slavic), púca (Celtic)

Polevik were typically depicted in white clothes

Gumiho

A gumiho was a supernatural shapeshifter from Korean folklore. It most commonly took the form of a nine–tailed fox, but could also change into a beautiful woman to attack men and feed on their hearts and livers.

Were usually depicted with its most distinguishing feature – the nine tails

Gumiho like me are foxes that have lived for 1,000 years, gaining the power of shapeshifting.

Super facts

Pronunciation: goo-mee-ho
Origin: Korean mythology **Location:** East Asia
Characteristic: Shapeshifting
Lookalikes: Dájǐ (Chinese), ho ly tinh (Vietnamese), húlíjīng (Chinese), Hú xiān (Chinese), kitsune (Japanese)

Dokkaebi

Dokkaebi were mythological Korean goblins and nature spirits that often used their exceptional powers to play pranks on people. They could also defend against evil spirits and bring humans great fortune.

Super facts

Pronunciation: DOH-keh-bee
Origin: Korean mythology
Location: East Asia
Characteristic: Shapeshifting
Lookalikes: Goblin (European), Huldufólk (Icelandic), oni (Japanese)

Although they could change form, Dokkaebi often appear as fearsome demons.

Its club, called the dokkaebi bangmangi, acted like a magic wand.

I love eating! My favourite foods are red bean rice cakes and buckwheat jelly.

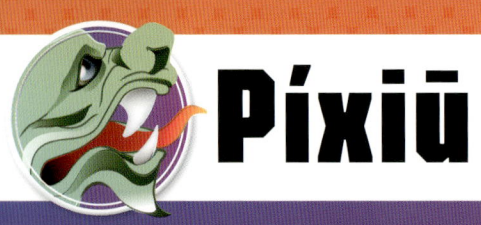

Píxiū

The Chinese píxiū looked fierce but was believed to bring good fortune. It was powerful in battle, destroyed evil spirits, and was said to have a body filled with gold.

Píxiū had the body of a lion and the head of a dragon.

Qílín

The qílín was a hooved, unicorn–like creature. It had the body of a deer and the tail of an ox. The qílín was said to only appear when an old ruler was about to die, or a new ruler born.

I am a very delicate creature. I never walk on grass or eat any living plants.

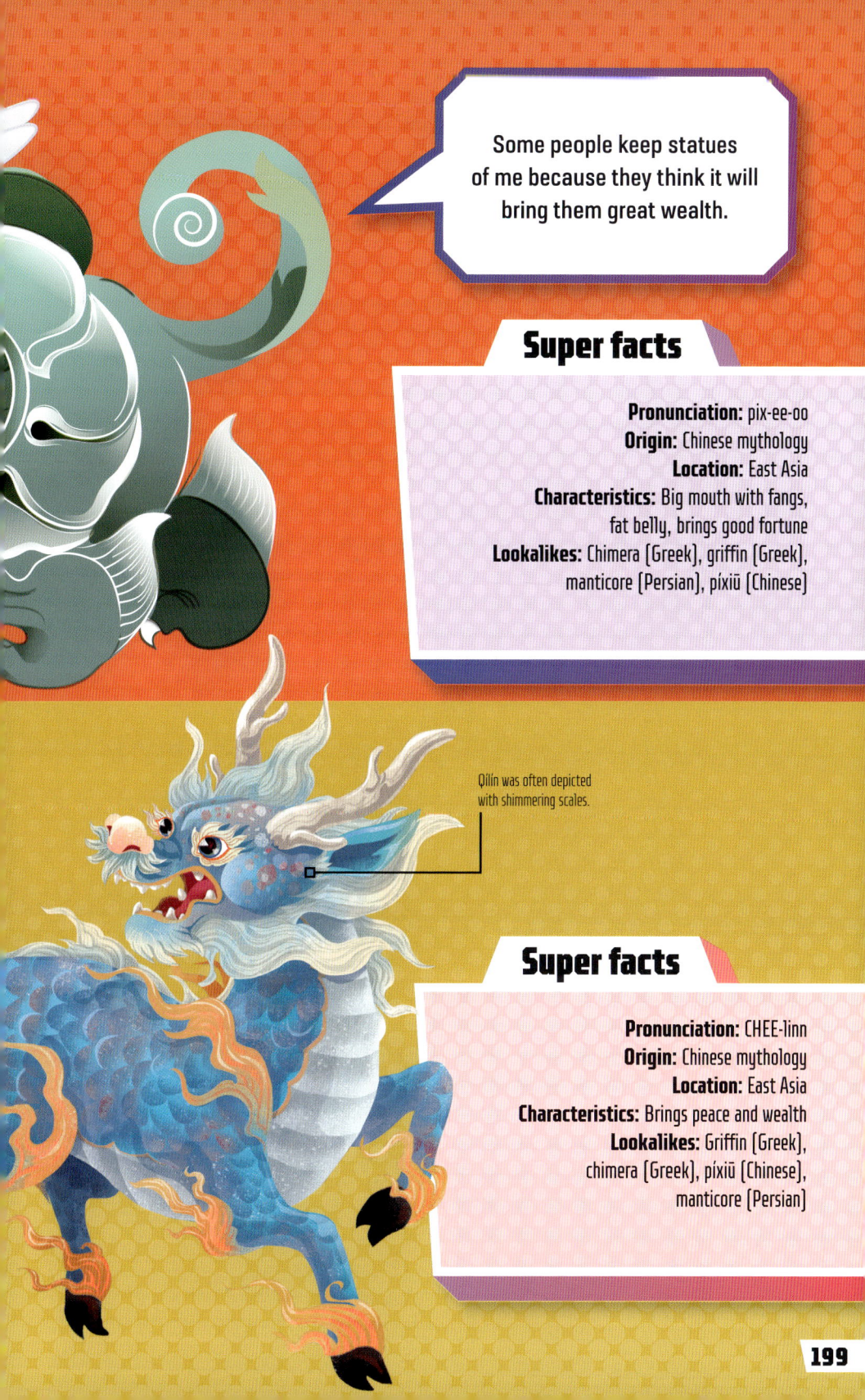

Some people keep statues of me because they think it will bring them great wealth.

Super facts

Pronunciation: pix-ee-oo
Origin: Chinese mythology
Location: East Asia
Characteristics: Big mouth with fangs, fat belly, brings good fortune
Lookalikes: Chimera (Greek), griffin (Greek), manticore (Persian), píxiū (Chinese)

Qilin was often depicted with shimmering scales.

Super facts

Pronunciation: CHEE-linn
Origin: Chinese mythology
Location: East Asia
Characteristics: Brings peace and wealth
Lookalikes: Griffin (Greek), chimera (Greek), píxiū (Chinese), manticore (Persian)

Legend of the Monkey King

Blessed with superhuman strength and shapeshifting skills, the Monkey King was a mischievous trickster from Chinese mythology. Also called Sūnwùkōng (*soon-woo-kong*), he was born from a magical rock, trained as a warrior, and wielded an eight-ton staff that could shrink to the size of a needle.

Mythical kingdoms

Often situated high in the heavens, mythical kingdoms were magical realms of gods and heroes. Sometimes divine paradises or walled fortresses, these kingdoms were usually remote, hidden places, inaccessible to mere mortals.

Shangri-la

Shangri-la was a lost, mythical Tibetan paradise, located somewhere in the Himalayan mountains. It was said to be built on a high plateau, with a lake and palace.

Lanka

Lanka was the gold-walled island fortress of the Hindu demon king Ravana. It was created when Ravana broke the top off a mountain and dropped it into the sea.

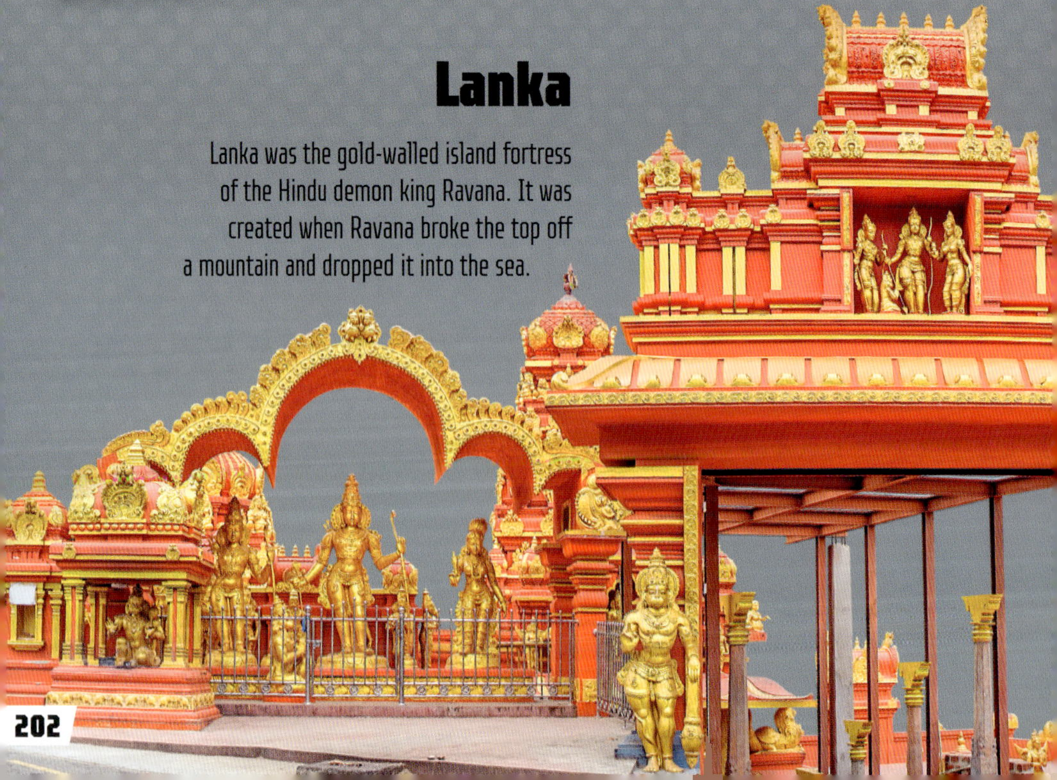

Asgard

Located at the top of the Norse universe, Asgard was home to the gods. Connected to the other eight worlds by the Bifrost bridge, Asgard was protected by a high wall.

The one-eyed god Odin watched over the Norse universe from his Asgardian palace, Valaskjalf (*val-a-skalf*).

Camelot

The legendary court of Britain's King Arthur, Camelot was a castle fortress said to contain a small city within its walls. It represented the ideals of chivalry, including courage, honour, and courtesy.

The Round Table of King Arthur's knights was situated in the grand hall of Camelot's castle.

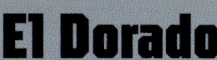

Tired travellers often imagined seeing a golden city shimmering in the distance.

El Dorado

According to legend, El Dorado was a city of gold that lay hidden in the mountains of South America. In the 16th century, Spanish explorers heard tales of it but never actually found it.

Shōjō

In Japanese folklore, shōjō were clever sea spirits who lived along the coast. They spent their time enjoying themselves and playing on the beach, and were kind to humans.

Shaggy red hair

We mostly stay away from people but sometimes we say hello and even know a few words in their language.

Super facts

Pronunciation: sho-joh
Meaning: Young girl
Origin: Japanese mythology
Location: East Asia
Characteristics: Reddish face, ape-like creature
Lookalikes: Nereid (Greek), selkie (Scottish), vodyanoy (Slavic)

Nuppeppō

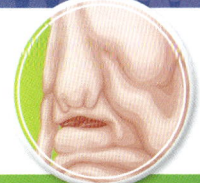

With a hideous appearance and an odour of rotting meat, nuppeppō were creepy creatures of Japanese folklore. They hung around in cemeteries but did not harm people – just disgusted passers-by.

I spend my time running around making people ill with my terrible smell and looks!

Flabby, humanoid form with lumpy, fleshy bits

Super facts

Pronunciation: noo-peh-po **Meaning:** Flat-faced
Origin: Japanese mythology **Location:** East Asia
Characteristics: Fleshy blob, lump-like arms, fat wrinkles **Lookalikes:** Aswang and manananggal (Filipino), fomorian (Irish)

Aghasura

Aghasura (*ah-GHA-soo-ra*) was an asura (demon) who fought for Kamsa, the tyrant ruler of the kingdom of Mathura. Kamsa and Aghasura both hated Krishna. In an attempt to kill him, Aghasura took the form of a serpent, measuring 13 km (8 miles) long, and opened his mouth wide, waiting for Krishna to walk inside.

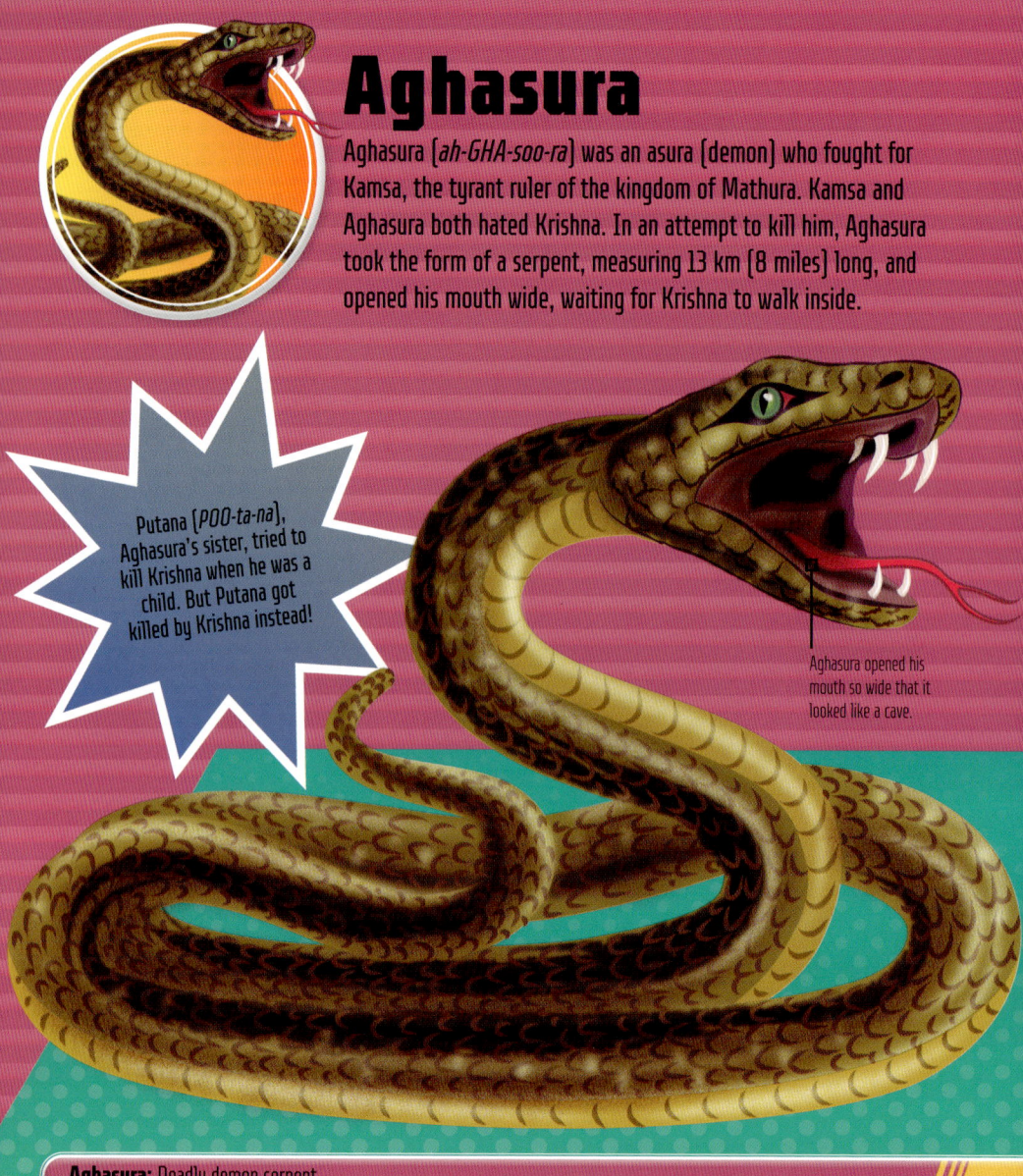

Putana (*POO-ta-na*), Aghasura's sister, tried to kill Krishna when he was a child. But Putana got killed by Krishna instead!

Aghasura opened his mouth so wide that it looked like a cave.

Aghasura: Deadly demon serpent

Battle up!

Aghasura was a demon sent by the Hindu king Kamsa to kill his enemy, Krishna. Aghasura's siblings had been slain by Krishna, so the demon jumped at the chance to travel to Earth and avenge his family.

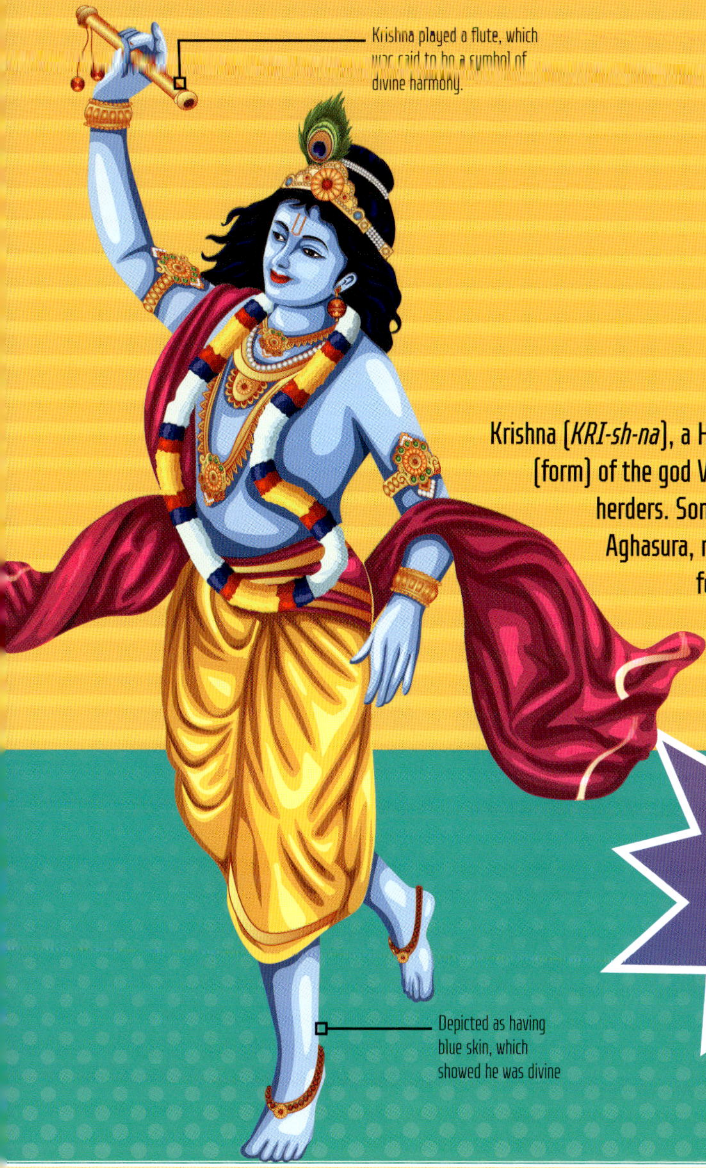

Krishna played a flute, which was said to be a symbol of divine harmony.

Krishna

Krishna (*KRI-sh-na*), a Hindu deity and human incarnation (form) of the god Vishnu, was raised on Earth by cow herders. Some of Krishna's friends, while near Aghasura, mistook the serpent's open mouth for a cave and walked inside as the demon lay in wait for Krishna.

Krishna, a beloved Hindu god, was known for his mischievous pranks.

Depicted as having blue skin, which showed he was divine

Krishna: Clever cowherd protector

Who wins?

Krishna saw his friends enter the cave and immediately realized it was Aghasura's mouth. He ran inside to free them. Krishna started to grow larger and larger until Aghasura started to choke. Eventually, Krishna burst out from the demon's head. Aghasura was dead, and Krishna's friends were safe!

Winner!

Golem

According to Jewish folklore, a golem (*GOH–lum*) was a small clay figure that could be made into a powerful being with a few magical phrases. While golems were obedient servants, they could be dangerous if left unchecked. In one story, a golem successfully protected a village from invaders but had to be watched closely afterwards, in case it ended up attacking the village itself.

Shapeshifters

Shapeshifters were supernatural beings that could transform themselves into other creatures or objects. Some shapeshifters began as humans and turned into wild animals, such as wolves. Others could shift between several different animals, such as goats, cats, and horses.

Tengu chiefs were often identified by their long, red noses.

Some tengu were able to summon fireballs.

Tengu

Supernatural creatures from Japanese folklore, tengu [*TENG-goo*] appeared as part-bird and part-human, and lived in trees. Tengu had magical powers and were master swordsmen, but spent most of their time simply playing tricks on people.

Cat Sith

A creature from Celtic mythology, the Cat Sith [*cat-SHEE*] was a fairy that could change into a cat nine times. The cat was the size of a dog, could stand on two legs, and would curse those who didn't leave out a saucer of milk for it.

Púca

The púca [*POO-ka*] were shapeshifters from Celtic folklore. They would change from human form into animals, such as goats and wolves. Then they made mischief, like taking people for rides on their backs only to abandon them later.

Kushtaka was sometimes called the Land-Otter Man.

Kushtaka

Shapeshifters of the folklore of Indigenous peoples of the Pacific Northwest, kushtaka [*koosh-ta-ka*] could take the form of an otter and lure victims into the deep forest. Once lost, it would feed on the person's soul.

Hanuman

Hanuman was a monkey god from Hindu mythology and a devoted servant of the highly worshipped deity Rama. He was famous for leading an army of monkeys to rescue Rama's wife, Sita, from the demon king Ravana.

Hanuman's main weapon was a gada (mace).

Did you know?
Hanuman once carried an entire mountain from the Himalayas to Lanka, so healing herbs could be picked from it.

Pronunciation: ha-noo-maan
Meaning: Prominent jaw
Origin: Hindu mythology
Location: South Asia
Characteristics: Flight, superstrength, tail, large jaw
Lookalikes: Monkey King (Chinese), Sugriva (Hindu)

When he was a young child, Hanuman tried to eat the Sun, which he thought was a fruit. Indra, the king of gods, threw a thunderbolt to stop him. The bolt struck him on the jaw, or Hanu, which is where he got his name from.

213

Moon Rabbit

In Chinese folklore, the Moon Rabbit lived on the Moon with the goddess Chang'e (*chang-uh*), and could be seen if people looked closely. Some stories say it produced the elixir of life potion, while others said it simply made rice cakes. The Moon Rabbit once travelled to Earth to help sick people. After that, it became a symbol for kindness and mystery.

Vampires

The classic vampire was a fanged creature that fed on human blood to survive. Variations of the vampire have existed in the myths, legends, and folklore of different cultures for hundreds of years.

Edimmu

In ancient Mesopotamian mythology, Edimmu [*eh-DEE-moo*] were the vengeful spirits of the dead that had not been properly buried. They would rise from their graves to possess people, and make them commit criminal acts.

Ghost-like creature

Dracula was often depicted sleeping in a coffin.

Dracula

Count Dracula [*DRAK-yuh-luh*] is a famous character with supernatural powers from Bram Stoker's 1897 horror novel, *Dracula*. It is said he shapeshifted into a bat and went out at night to drink human blood. Dracula was partly based on the 15th-century Transylvanian prince, Vlad the Impaler.

Peuchen

Found in Chilean mythology, the Peuchen [*pay-oo-CHEN*] was a shapeshifting vampire that could take the form of a flying serpent. The Peuchen was believed to paralyse its victims with one look, so it could suck their blood easily.

Often depicted with shimmering scales

Mandurugo used their sharp tongues to suck blood from victims.

Mandurugo

Mandurugo [*man-doo-ROO-go*] were shapeshifting vampires from Filipino folklore. They appeared as beautiful women during the day and turned into winged monsters at night.

Sometimes shown as a woman wearing traditional African clothes and headdress

Ramanga

A vampire from the folklore of Madagascar, Africa, the Ramanga [*rah-MAHN-gah*] was a fearsome creature. It only drank the blood of nobles or other high-ranking people and even ate their nail clippings.

Abada

Abada was a unicorn–type creature from the mythology of the Democratic Republic of Congo. However, unlike other unicorns, it had two horns on its head instead of one.

> I am known as a guide and protector of people.

The Abada was thought to be around the size of a donkey.

Super facts

Pronunciation: aba-da
Origin: Kongo mythology
Location: Central Africa
Characteristics: Two crooked horns, healing powers
Lookalikes: Sleipnir (Norse), unicorn (Hindu and Chinese)

Ammit

Ammit was a ferocious Egyptian beast who lived in the underworld. She would wait in the Hall of Judgement while a person's heart was weighed against a feather. If the heart was heavier than the feather, Ammit would gobble it up.

Super facts

Pronunciation: AM-mit
Origin: Egyptian mythology
Location: Egypt and northeastern Africa
Characteristics: Head of a crocodile, forelegs of a lion, back of a hippopotamus
Lookalikes: Cipactli (Aztec), Sobek (Egyptian),

Head of a crocodile

Back of a hippopotamus

Thoth, the Egyptian god of wisdom and the Moon, feeds me the hearts of sinners. I am often called "the devourer" by people.

Khepri

Khepri (*KEH-pree*) was the Egyptian beetle god who represented the rising Sun and its journey as a solar disc across the sky. He was almost certainly inspired by the dung beetle, which rolls balls of dung along the ground. The god was often depicted as a man with the head of a beetle.

Giants

Giants appeared in most mythologies from around the world. Some were like huge humans, with savage tempers and supernatural strength. Others were multiheaded, hairy monsters. Many giants had a taste for human flesh.

Oni

Oni (*oh-nee*) were giant demons from Japanese mythology. They were said to swoop down on people about to die and steal their souls. Some oni hunted down sinners and took them to hell in their chariots of fire.

Div were usually shown with hairy bodies.

Div

Massive monsters with multiple heads, horns, and boar-tusk teeth, div (*deev*) were giants from Persian mythology. Cruel creatures, they wielded large stones as weapons and fed on human flesh.

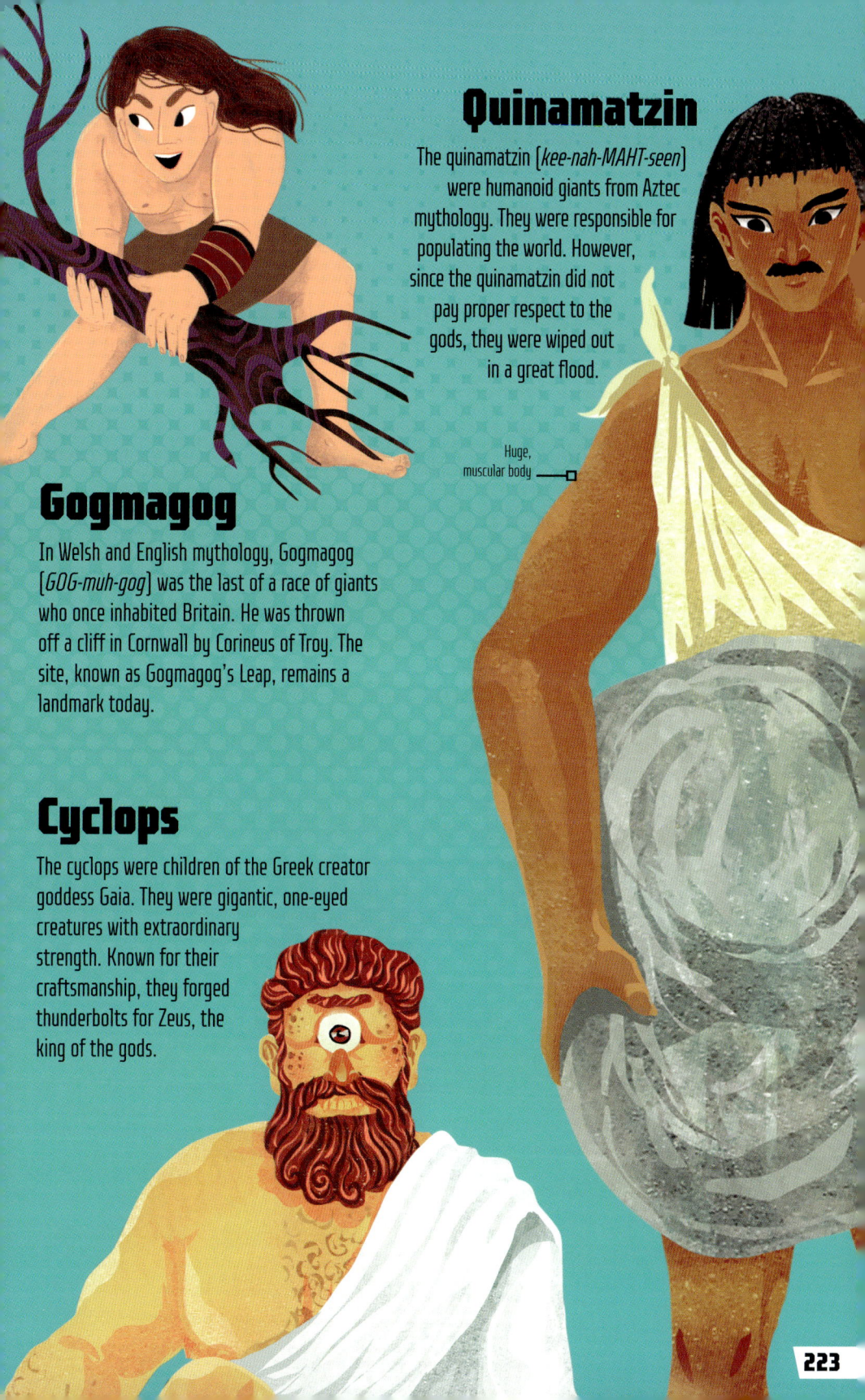

Quinamatzin

The quinamatzin [*kee-nah-MAHT-seen*] were humanoid giants from Aztec mythology. They were responsible for populating the world. However, since the quinamatzin did not pay proper respect to the gods, they were wiped out in a great flood.

Huge, muscular body

Gogmagog

In Welsh and English mythology, Gogmagog [*GOG-muh-gog*] was the last of a race of giants who once inhabited Britain. He was thrown off a cliff in Cornwall by Corineus of Troy. The site, known as Gogmagog's Leap, remains a landmark today.

Cyclops

The cyclops were children of the Greek creator goddess Gaia. They were gigantic, one-eyed creatures with extraordinary strength. Known for their craftsmanship, they forged thunderbolts for Zeus, the king of the gods.

Abaia

In Melanesian mythology, Abaia was a large, magical eel that lived at the bottom of a lake. It protected the lake's creatures and could control the weather, storms, and floods.

Super facts

Pronunciation: ah-bah-ee-ah
Origin: Melanesian mythology
Location: Oceania in the southwestern Pacific Ocean
Characteristics: Iridescent scales, gleaming eyes
Lookalikes: Inkanyamba (Africa), Jörmungandr (Norse), Taniwha (Māori)

A well-known story about Abaia tells of a fisherman who caught it in a net along with other fish. However, Abaia escaped and punished those who ate the fish by bringing a great rain that drowned them.

Abaia was said to have a thick, long body.

Gleaming eyes

Did you know?
Some people believed that a lake in Papua New Guinea, was home to Abaia.

Oozlum

Popular in British and Australian folklore, the Oozlum bird is a strange creature that flies backwards so it can admire its own tail feathers. It is said that by flying in smaller and smaller circles, it could eventually disappear.

Beautiful, multicoloured feathers

I was first written about by William Thomas Goodge, a 19th-century English poet, who said he saw me flying in Australia.

Super facts

Pronunciation: OOZ-luhm
Origin: British and Australian folklore
Location: England, Wales, Scotland, and Australia
Characteristics: Wise, flies tail first to keep dust out of its eyes, can fly backwards
Lookalikes: Jatayu (Hindu), raven (Norse)

Yowie

Similar to Bigfoot, the Yowie of the Australian outback has large feet, is covered with hair, and is taller than an ape. The creature was first spotted in the 18th century, but people still claim to see it today.

Super facts

Pronunciation: YOW-ee
Origin: First Australian mythology
Location: Australia
Characteristics: Bat-like ears, long arms, large hands, hairy
Lookalikes: Bigfoot (North American), hsigo (Chinese), yeti (Asian)

Also known as the "hairy man" by First Australian peoples

I am a frightening being and will steal children away if they are found in the bush after dark.

Dirawong

Taking the form of a giant Goanna lizard, the Dirawong was an ancestral creature from the First Australian mythology. It lived in the world when time began and was known as the guardian of the land and the teacher of people.

Super facts

Pronunciation: dira-wong
Origin: First Australian mythology
Location: Southeastern Australia
Characteristics: Ancestral being, magical spirit, scales that shimmer in the shades of the outback
Lookalikes: Basilisk (European), mo'o (Hawaiian), Taniwha (Māori)

The Dirawong once fought an epic battle with the Rainbow Serpent, an immortal being that could create life. As the giant creatures wrestled, their thrashing bodies carved out rivers and islands around Australia's New South Wales.

Long neck

Did you know?
The Dirawong once single-handedly fought off an invasion of sea creatures to protect the people on shore.

Tricksters

Tricksters were clever, cunning, and entertaining troublemakers. They were usually gods, goddesses, or supernatural creatures, who loved to play pranks and break the rules. Tricksters often seemed foolish and amusing, but they could also be disruptive and harmful.

Coyote

Coyote [*KAI-oh-tee*] was a shapeshifting god from the stories of the Indigenous peoples of the Pacific Northwest. In one story, he gave humans the gift of fire. In another, he turned himself into a chopping board to steal food being prepared on it.

Kitsune

Kitsune [kee-tsoo-neh] is the Japanese word for fox, but Kitsune were also supernatural foxes from Japanese mythology that lived for hundreds of years! Either helpful or mysterious, they could change shape and possess the bodies of humans.

Kitsune either appeared as humans, or foxes with large, luxurious tails.

Blue-tongue lizard

According to the stories of the First Australian people, the Blue-tongue lizard was a trickster deity. He pretended to be blind so his sons would bring him food. But when his sons killed a magical kangaroo, the Blue-tongue lizard cursed them with fire, which burned them alive.

Māui

A trickster demigod from Polynesian mythology, Māui once captured the Sun to make the days longer. He also stole fire as a gift for humans. It is said that Māui snuck onto his brothers' canoe and fished up the North Island of New Zealand.

Māui was shown holding the jawbone of his grandmother, which he used as a fishing hook.

Heroes, villains, and monsters

Heroes, villains, and monsters represent the light and darkness of mythology, as well as the terror of the unknown. Brave heroes lived and died by the sword, while villains hatched evil plans to destroy them. Meanwhile, monsters lurked in the deep, dark places of the world, waiting for a perfect moment to unleash themselves.

Achilles

The son of King Peleus (*PEH–lee-uss*) and the sea nymph Thetis (*THEH-tiss*), Achilles was the greatest of the Greek warriors. Brave, handsome, and unmatched on the battlefield, he played a key role in the Trojan War.

Super facts

Pronunciation: aa-KIL-eez
Meaning: He who has the people distressed
Origin: Greek mythology
Location: Greece and western coast of Türkiye (Turkey)
Characteristics: Extraordinarily strong, courageous, loyal
Associations: Hector, Patroclus, Phthia, Peleus

Thetis tried to make Achilles immortal by dipping him in the River Styx, a river in the underworld that had magical properties. However, Achilles's heel did not enter the water and remained vulnerable. Later, Achilles was killed when the Trojan prince, Paris, shot an arrow into his heel.

Achilles was shown as a tall man with long hair.

Made by Hephaestus, the god of fire, Achilles's armour was the finest ever created.

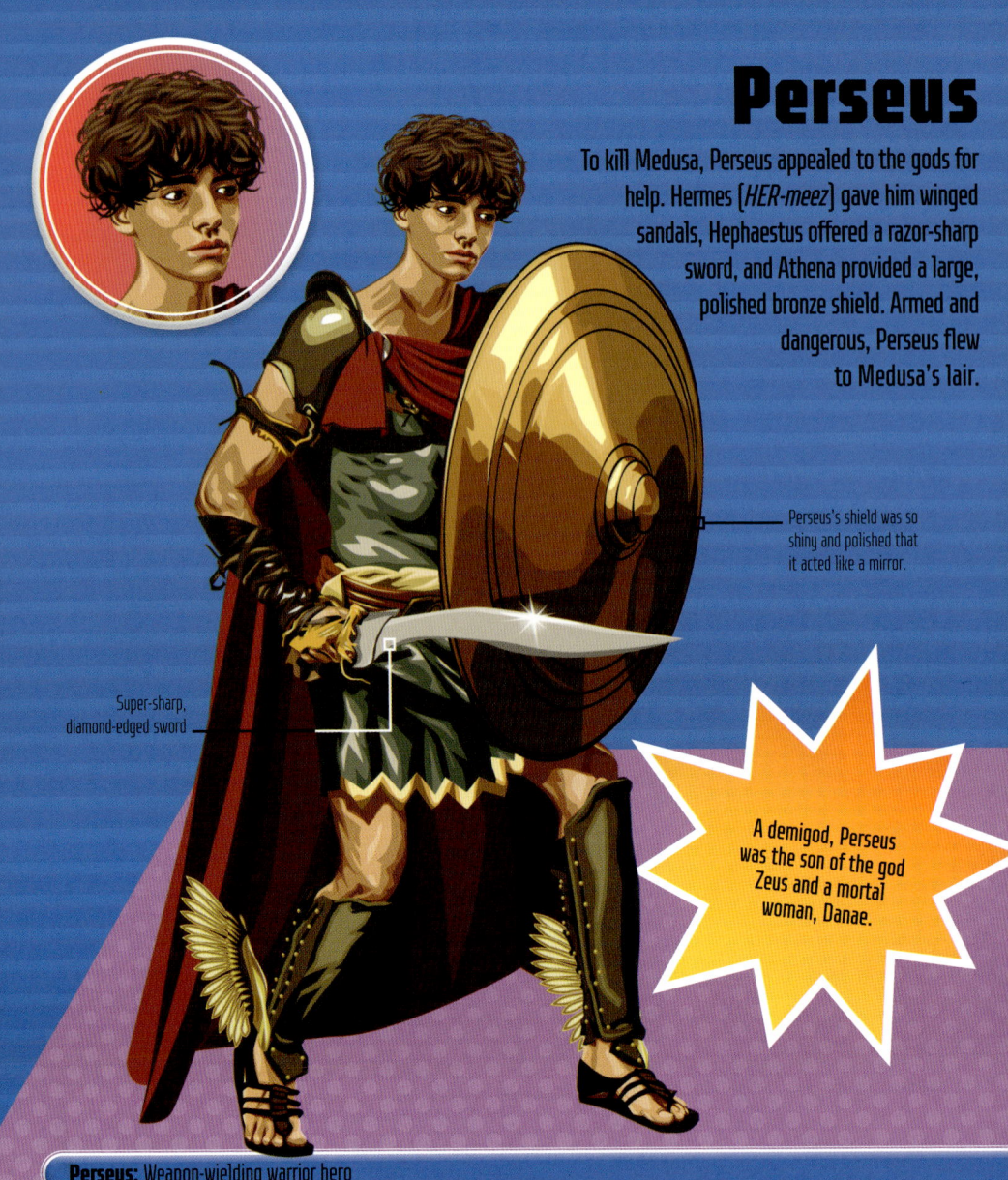

Perseus

To kill Medusa, Perseus appealed to the gods for help. Hermes (*HER-meez*) gave him winged sandals, Hephaestus offered a razor-sharp sword, and Athena provided a large, polished bronze shield. Armed and dangerous, Perseus flew to Medusa's lair.

Perseus's shield was so shiny and polished that it acted like a mirror.

Super-sharp, diamond-edged sword

A demigod, Perseus was the son of the god Zeus and a mortal woman, Danae.

Perseus: Weapon-wielding warrior hero

Battle up!

At dinner one day, the Greek king Polydectes (*poli–DEK-tees*) of Seriphos asked his guests what gifts they could give him. His adopted son, Perseus bragged that he could bring him the head of the monster known as the Medusa.

Medusa

One of three female monsters called the gorgons (*GOR-gon*), Medusa was a terrifying creature with snakes for hair. Her face was so hideous that it turned anyone who gazed upon it to stone. Her lair was littered with the stone remains of those who had stared at her.

Writhing snakes sat upon Medusa's head in place of hair.

Was sometimes depicted with green skin

Medusa was once a beautiful woman, but the goddess Athena cursed her to become a gorgon.

Medusa: Snake-haired monster

Who wins?

As Perseus approached Medusa, he tilted his shield so he could see her reflection in it. This stopped him from looking Medusa directly in the eye, so she couldn't turn him to stone. He was then able to cut off her head. Incredibly, the flying horse Pegasus flew out of Medusa's bloody neck.

Winner!

The Amazons

According to ancient Greek mythology, the Amazons were a fierce race of warrior women who lived far from other civilizations. They were skilled in using bows, spears, axes, and other weapons. When the Amazons had children, they only raised the girls, while the boys were sent away with their fathers.

Labours of Heracles

The greatest Greek hero, Heracles (*HEH–ra–kleez*) was a powerful demigod and the son of Zeus. But he was tricked into killing his wife and children and had to perform 12 difficult tasks as punishment. These were known as the Labours of Heracles.

Heracles

Before the labours, Heracles was already famous for his strength and bravery. He had even joined the Argonauts (*AH-goh-nort*), a group of brave heroes, on their quest to find the Golden Fleece.

1. Nemean lion

The first task was to slay the Nemean lion, but its skin could not be pierced by arrows. Heracles clubbed and strangled the lion and then took its hide (skin).

2. The Hydra

The Hydra was a nine-headed snake whose heads regrew after being cut off. To slay the Hydra, Heracles had to burn its necks after chopping off each head.

3. Golden Hind

The Golden Hind ran faster than a speeding arrow. Heracles had to chase it across Greece for a year before finally catching it in his net.

4. The boar
Catching the destructive Erymanthian boar was Heracles's fourth task. He chased it into a snowdrift and threw it into the sea.

5. Augean stables
Heracles was given one day to clean the Augean stables that housed thousands of animals. He diverted two rivers to run through the stables and clean them.

6. Stymphalian birds
To clear a big flock of birds bothering a town, Heracles used noisemaking clappers made by the god Hephaestus and shot the birds as they fled.

7. Cretan bull
The seventh task was to catch a mad, wild bull rampaging across Crete. Heracles ambushed the bull, wrestled it to the ground, and then wrapped it in chains.

8. Mares of Diomedes
To capture human-eating mares, Heracles killed their owner, Diomedes, and fed his flesh to the horses. This gave him time to tie the animals up.

9. Belt of Hippolyta
Heracles was then asked to obtain the magical belt of Hippolyta, the queen of the Amazons. He had to kill Hippolyta to complete this task.

10. Geryon's cattle
To steal the cattle from Geryon, a three-headed giant, Heracles had to first kill the giant's guard dog and then Geryon.

11. Golden apples
For his eleventh task, Heracles asked Atlas to get the golden apples. He held the world for Atlas, then tricked him into taking it back.

12. Cerberus
For his final task, Heracles had to capture Cerberus, the multiheaded dog from the underworld. He did so by sweeping him up in his cloak.

Valkyrie

Super facts

Pronunciation: VAL-ki-ree
Meaning: Chooser of the slain
Origin: Norse mythology
Location: North Atlantic and northern Europe
Characteristics: Power to cause the death of warriors, always female
Associations: Odin, Viking warriors

Valkyries were Odin's female spirits. They swooped over battlefields and picked dead, heroic warriors to join the god in his hall of Valhalla.

We greet dead warriors at the hall of Valhalla with a horn of mead. They then prepare for the battle of Ragnarök.

Valkyries were often shown as warriors on horses.

Brunhild

Brunhild was one of Odin's Valkyries until she refused the god's orders on the battlefield. Odin then turned her into a mortal woman and placed her into a deep sleep.

Only a true hero could rouse me from my deep slumber. I was finally woken up by the hero-warrior Sigurd (*sig-urd*).

Brunhild was usually depicted with a mighty shield.

Super facts

Pronunciation: BREEN-hild
Meaning: Battle armour
Origin: Norse mythology
Location: North Atlantic and northern Europe
Characteristics: Headstrong, female warrior
Associations: Odin, Valkyries

Sigurd

A warrior of the Volsung family, Sigurd was given an unbreakable sword, called Gram, by the blacksmith Regin. In return, Sigurd agreed to kill the dragon Fafnir.

Flameproof metal shield

Sigurd's sword, Gram, was made from a broken sword that once belonged to the god Odin.

Sigurd comes from the old Norse word *Sigurðr*, meaning "victory" and "guard".

Sigurd: Mighty dragon slayer

Battle up!

Sigurd was a legendary Norse hero who had once promised the blacksmith Regin that he would slay the dragon Fafnir. Now, he prepared to fulfil this promise.

Fafnir

Fafnir (*faf-neer*) was Regin's brother who had once been human. However, he tricked Regin over a treasure hoard and then turned into a greedy dragon. Regin now wanted him dead.

Fafnir was a winged dragon sometimes called a firedrake.

Fafnir killed his father, Hreidmar, and tricked his brother Regin for the treasure. This immense greed for treasure is called dragon sickness!

Fafnir: Flaming firedrake

Who wins?

Sigurd dug a large hole in the path between Fafnir's lair and a nearby river. Then he lay in the hole and waited. When Fafnir slithered down the path to drink water, Sigurd stabbed him in the heart. The dragon was dead!

Winner!

King Arthur

King Arthur was a legendary king of Britain who ruled from the mythical Camelot. He was the head of the Knights of the Round Table. Arthur might have been a real king who fought against Anglo–Saxons in the 5th century CE.

King Arthur was usually shown wielding his famous sword, Excalibur.

I feature in many tales about Camelot, including the ones about Queen Guinevere and my best knight, Lancelot.

Super facts

Pronunciation: AH-thur
Meaning: Of honour
Origin: British folklore
Location: England, Wales, and Scotland
Characteristics: Brave knight and warrior, fair king
Associations: Merlin, Knights of the Round Table

Merlin

Merlin was the mythical magician of Camelot and adviser to King Arthur. He suggested that the king and his knights go in search of the Holy Grail, a lost, sacred cup.

Super facts

Pronunciation: mer-linn
Meaning: Sea pool
Origin: British folklore
Location: England, Wales, and Scotland
Characteristics: Wise, magician, shapeshifter
Associations: King Arthur, Lady of the Lake

Often depicted with a long staff

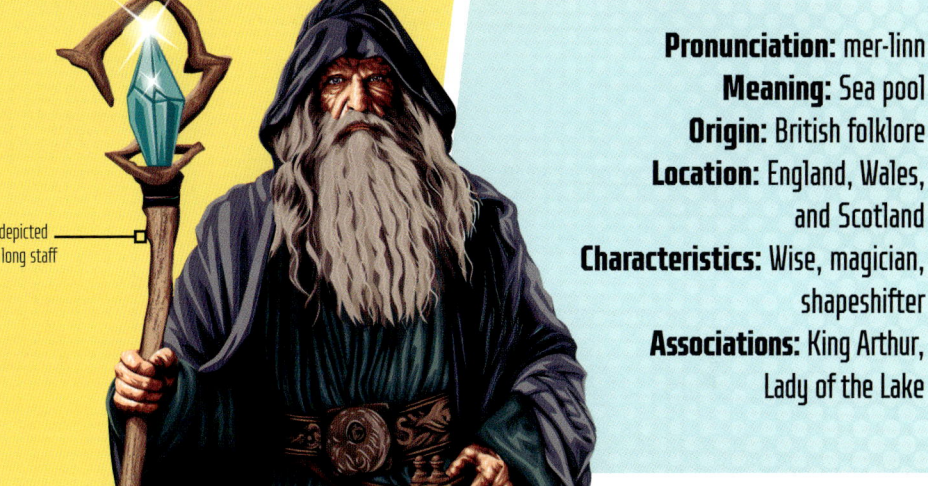

I showed Arthur the "sword in the stone", which he pulled out to become king!

Beowulf

Beowulf (*bay-uh-wulf*), the prince of the Geats, was welcomed in Hrothgar's hall with a grand celebration. That night when Grendel ripped open the hall's door to eat a sleeping warrior, Beowulf was ready to fight him.

Beowulf was a powerful warrior who wore a helmet.

After battling Grendel, Beowulf travelled home and became King of the Geats.

Beowulf: The bare-handed battler

Battle up!

For 12 long years, the evil monster Grendel had been breaking into the hall of the Danish king Hrothgar (*hrawth-gar*) and devouring his warriors. When the news reached the Swedish hero Beowulf, he offered to come and battle the monster.

Grendel

Grendel (*gren-dl*) was a strong swamp monster who had once again come to kill Hrothgar's men. However, this time he had to face Beowulf. After a deadly fight, the Swedish hero tore off Grendel's arm. Mortally wounded, Grendel stumbled back to the swamp to die.

Grendel's reptilian skin was so tough that it could not be pierced by a blade.

Skin covered in rock-hard scales

Grendel: The man-eating monster

Who wins?

While the warriors celebrated the end of Grendel in Hrothgar's hall, another swamp monster ambushed them. It was Grendel's mother. Seeking revenge, she killed a warrior before rushing away. Beowulf chased her down to her cave, and slayed her. The monsters were finally all gone!

Winner!

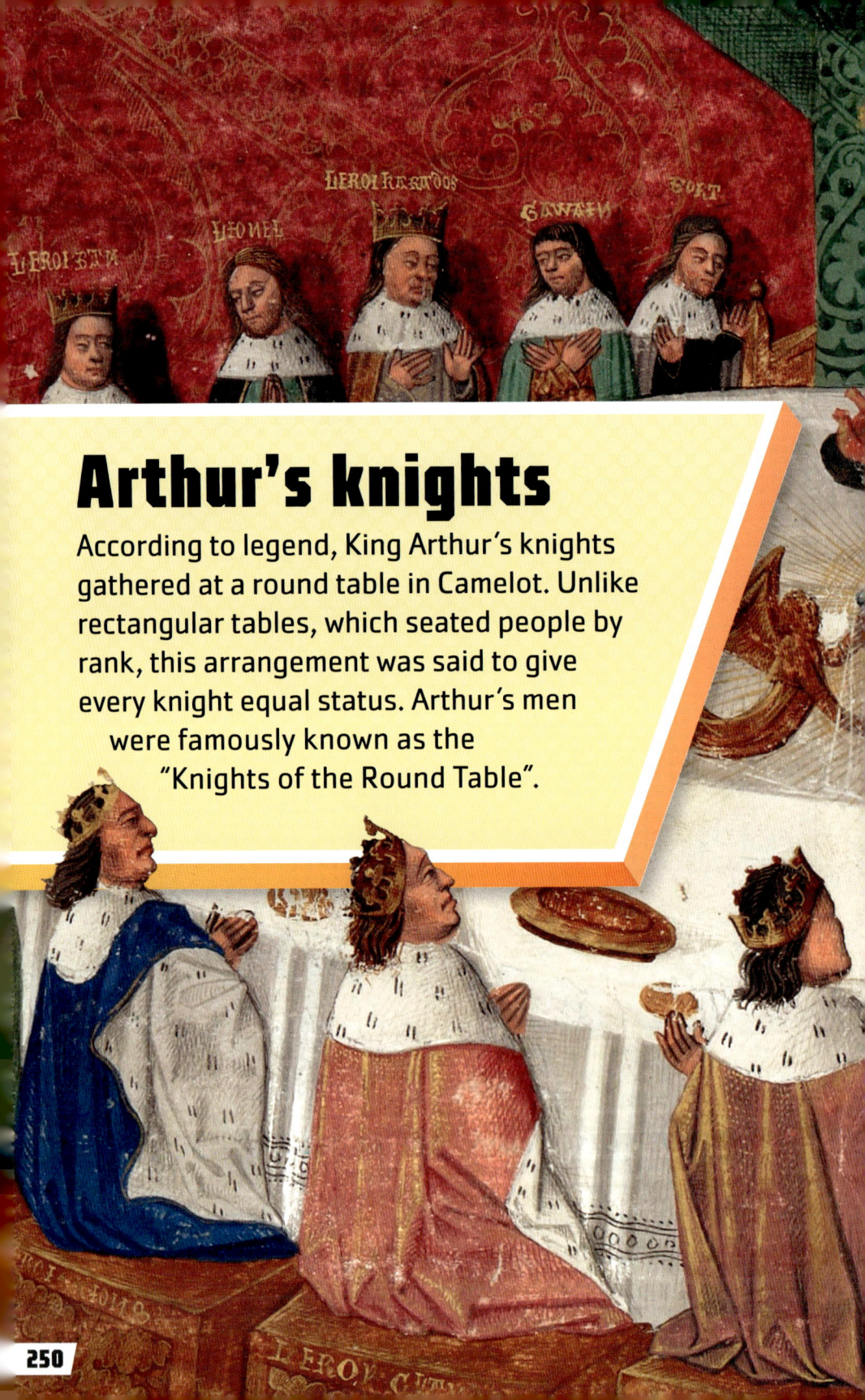

Arthur's knights

According to legend, King Arthur's knights gathered at a round table in Camelot. Unlike rectangular tables, which seated people by rank, this arrangement was said to give every knight equal status. Arthur's men were famously known as the "Knights of the Round Table".

Gilgamesh

Gilgamesh was the legendary king of Uruk, a city in Mesopotamia in the 3rd century BCE. According to the ancient poem the *Epic of Gilgamesh*, he was a cruel, tyrannical ruler who wanted to live forever.

Super facts

Pronunciation: GILL-ga-mesh
Meaning: The old man is a young man
Origin: Mesopotamian mythology
Location: Southwestern Asia
Characteristics: Great builder, skilled warrior
Association: Enkidu

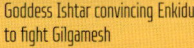

Goddess Ishtar convincing Enkidu to fight Gilgamesh

To control Gilgamesh's power, the gods sent the wild man Enkidu (*EN-kee-doo*) to challenge him. The two fought for days, but neither could win so they became friends. In the end, the gods had to kill Enkidu, as he was such a bad influence.

Did you know?
Gilgamesh discovered an underwater plant that could grant immortality, but a snake snatched it away. Accepting his mortality, he resolved to become a better ruler.

Was usually shown with a lion to demonstrate his strength.

Yamato Takeru

The heroic son of Japanese Emperor Kiekō, Yamato Takeru was a legendary warrior prince. He was known to assassinate bandits and crush rebels as commanded by his father.

> I disguised myself as a woman to gain entry to a bandits banquet. When they became drunk, I slayed them.

Mostly shown wearing warrior clothes from 2nd-century Japan

Usually carried a sword

Super facts

Pronunciation: yah-mah-toe tah-keh-roo
Meaning: Great harmony   **Origin:** Japanese folklore   **Location:** East Asia
Characteristics: Warrior, courageous, cunning
Associations: Emperor Keikō, Princess Ototachibana

Yorimitsu

Yorimitsu, a leading member of the Minamoto clan, was a legendary samurai warrior. Along with his four sidekicks, he went on many quests, and their exploits are famously remembered in Japanese folklore.

Was usually depicted with a katana sword

Super facts

Pronunciation: your-im-it-soo
Meaning: To depend on
Origin: Japanese folklore
Location: East Asia
Characteristics: Agile, courageous, warrior, protector
Associations: Sakata no Kintoki, Urabe Suetake, Usui Sadamitsu, Watanabe no Tsuna

My warriors and I once disguised ourselves as priests to kill a giant feasting on human blood. Even after the giant was beheaded, his head kept attacking us!

Shuten-dōji

Shuten-dōji (*shoo-TEN-doh-jee*) was a giant demon who ruled over a gang of bandits and criminals. They would ride out from Shuten-dōji's castle to feed on human flesh and blood, and perform black magic rituals.

Shuten-dōji was sometimes depicted with the body of a giant.

Shuten-dōji, a fierce demon, was often called "Little Drunkard," as he was known to drink a lot of alcohol.

Shuten-dōji: Demonic human-eater

Battle up!

Shuten–dōji was an evil demon who roamed the Japanese countryside, devouring humans. Only a legendary warrior could stop him. Step forth, Kintarō!

Kintarō

Kintarō (*kin-ta-ro*) was born a golden child with superhuman strength. He was kind and noble, and even as a child, his heroic deeds became legendary. As he grew older, he was invited to join the Four Braves, an elite group of samurai warriors.

Kintarō was often shown with an axe – he could chop down whole trees at the age of eight.

Kintarō was often depicted with the plump, reddish face of a toddler.

Kintarō: Wonder-boy warrior

Who wins?

Kintarō and the Four Braves dressed up as monks to gain entry into Shuten-dōji's castle. They got Shuten-dōji's thugs drunk and then attacked. Even though Kintarō chopped off Shuten-dōji's head, the demon continued to attack him. In the end, however, Kintarō and the Four Braves won the battle.

Winner!

Hua Mulan

A heroine from Chinese folklore, Hua Mulan disguised herself as a man and joined the army at the age of 17. She went on to become one of the emperor's most powerful and important warriors.

Usually dressed in traditional military uniform

Did you know?
After 12 years in the army, Hua Mulan returned home and revealed she was a woman, much to the astonishment of her fellow soldiers.

Super facts

Pronunciation: hwah MOO-lan
Meaning: Magnolia
Origin: Chinese mythology   **Location:** East Asia
Characteristics: Brave warrior, remarkable combat skills
Associations: Emperor, fellow soldiers, General Li Jing

Mulan's story has been told in many ways over the years. It started with a 7th-century poem called *The Ballad of Mulan*, based on a brave woman warrior. Today, her story is also performed on stage by dancers.

An arrow shot from Rama's bow never missed its target.

Rama's magical bow, called Sharanga (*sha-run-gah*), once belonged to the god Vishnu.

Rama

A widely worshipped Hindu deity, Rama (*ra-ma*) had a reputation as a great warrior. Stringing the bow that belonged to the god Shiva earned Rama his marriage to Sita. A skilled archer, he defeated a group of disruptive demons with his magical bow.

Rama was considered the most wise, moral, and virtuous (good) child of King Dasharatha and Queen Kaushalya.

Rama: Warrior-deity and hero husband

Battle up!

In the Hindu epic (long poem) *Ramayana*, the demon king Ravana abducted Sita, the wife of Rama. Ravana imprisoned Sita on his island kingdom of Lanka. Rama immediately set out to rescue his wife and rid the world of Ravana's evil deeds.

Ravana wielded a large, indestructible sword that was given to him by the god Shiva

Ravana

The 10-headed king of the demons, Ravana (*ra-vah-nah*) could change into any form and was strong enough to throw entire mountains. It was said Ravana could only be killed by a mortal man.

To stop Ravana from constantly shaking Mount Kailash, the god Shiva placed his toe on the mountain, trapping Ravana underneath for 1,000 years.

Ravana: Multiheaded demon king

Who wins?

The monkey god Hanuman helped Rama by ordering his army to build a bridge to the island of Lanka. Once the battle began, Rama attacked Ravana and cut off his heads, but they kept growing back. Ravana was finally defeated when Rama shot an arrow at his navel, his weak spot.

Winner!

Urduja

Urduja was a legendary warrior princess who ruled over a 14th–century kingdom in the Philippines. A fierce fighter, Urduja commanded an army of both men and women.

Super facts

Pronunciation: ur-DOO-ja
Meaning: Rising sun
Origin: Pangasinan folklore   **Location:** Philippines
Characteristics: Warrior, skilled navigator, expert in weaponry, leader
Association: Ibn Battuta

The ADVENTURES of IBN BATTUTA
A Muslim Traveler of the 14th Century
ROSS E. DUNN

According to the writings of Arab traveller Ibn Battuta, Urduja was a real princess who fought in duels. It is said that Urduja declared she would only marry the man who could defeat her. As such, she remained unmarried for her whole life.

She was shown dressed as a Filipino warrior.

Did you know?
Urduja was said to welcome customs and cuisine from other countries and adopt them into her own. She could speak many languages.

Carried a sword

Jinns

Also known as djinns, jinns were invisible, supernatural spirits in Asian and Middle Eastern folklore. They dwelled in many places, from rocks to fire, and could appear in animal and human forms. Some jinns could grant wishes, while others caused harm.

Iblis

Iblis [*ib-lees*] was a devil who was originally thrown out of heaven for not bowing before god. He then became the father of the jinns.

According to modern folklore, hinn often appeared as dogs.

Hinn

Related to jinns, the hinn were supernatural beings that existed before humans. They later took the form of dogs. At one time, the hinn fought alongside angels in heaven.

Vetala

Vetala (*vey-tah-lah*) was a strange spirit that haunted cemeteries and morgues. It could possess the bodies of dead people and was considered dangerous and evil.

Vetala is most commonly shown as a "reanimated corpse", called a zombie.

Marid

Most commonly associated with genies, the marid were giant jinns that could change their appearance and grant wishes. However, wishes could only be granted by fighting or flattering a Marid.

Nasnas

Born from human and jinn parents, the Nasnas was a creature made from one side of a human. It had half a body, half a head, one arm, and one leg, which it hopped around on.

Makwa Bimose

In the folklore of Indigenous peoples of the Pacific Northwest, Makwa Bimose, or the bear walker, was a human sorcerer who could shapeshift into a bear to carry out evil deeds. Bear walkers could paralyse people, or bring sickness and death upon them.

> I walk by night to bring danger to all who see me.

Usually shown as a large bear standing on two feet

Super facts

Pronunciation: MAHK-wah BEE-moh-say
Origin: Folklore of Indigenous peoples of the Pacific Northwest   **Location:** North America
Characteristics: Shapeshifting, superstrength

Wendigo

The wendigo was a strong, terrifying spirit that fed on human flesh. It could also turn people into cannibals, so they ate one another.

I was once a lost hunter who became so hungry that I had to kill my companions for food.

Super facts

Pronunciation: WEN-dee-go
Origin: Folklore of Indigenous peoples of the Pacific Northwest
Location: North America
Characteristics: Pale, skinny, sunken eyes, greedy, cruel

A giant beast with sharp claws

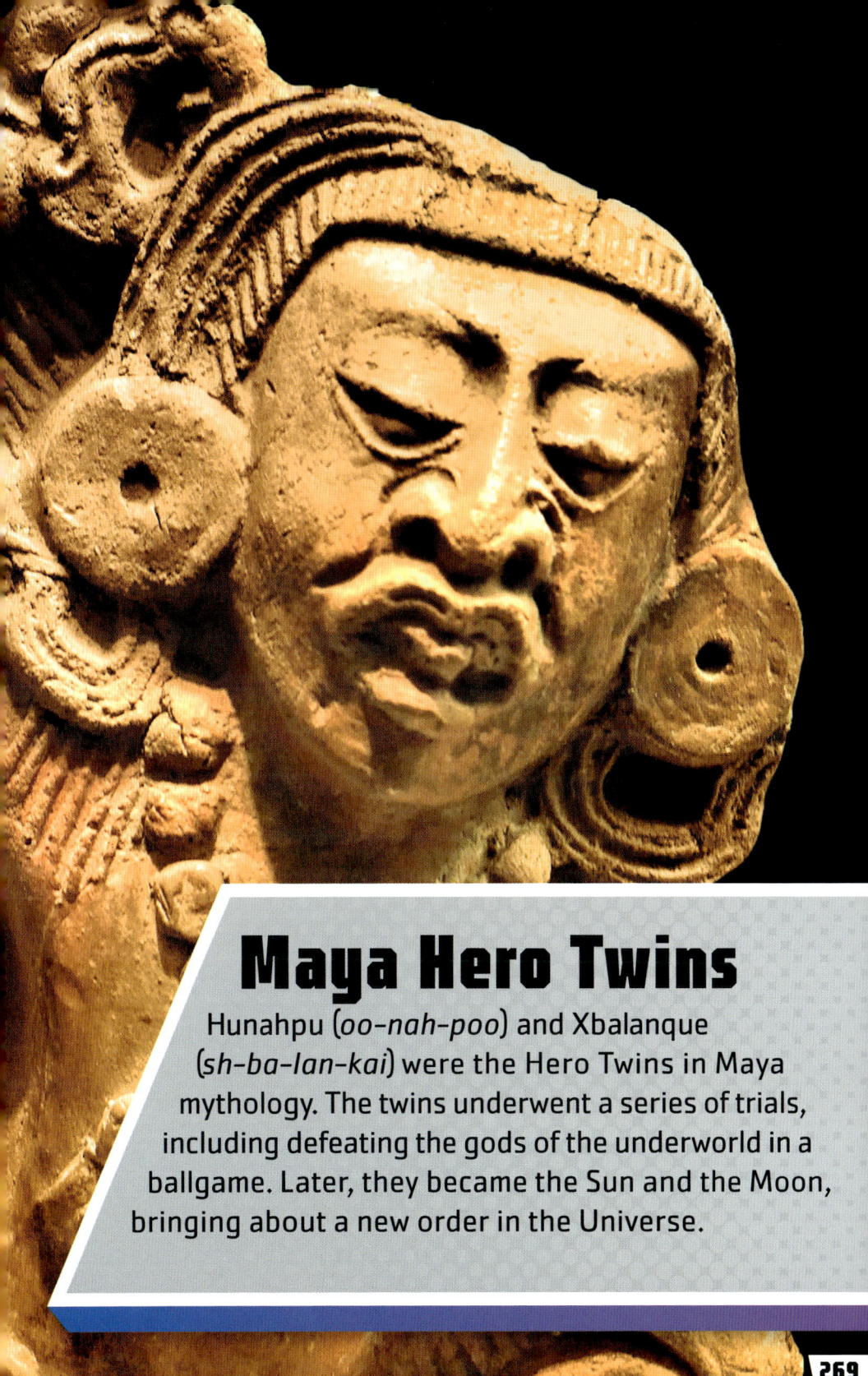

Maya Hero Twins

Hunahpu (*oo-nah-poo*) and Xbalanque (*sh-ba-lan-kai*) were the Hero Twins in Maya mythology. The twins underwent a series of trials, including defeating the gods of the underworld in a ballgame. Later, they became the Sun and the Moon, bringing about a new order in the Universe.

Kholomodumo

Super facts

Pronunciation: KOH-loh-moh-DOO-moh
Origin: Sotho mythology
Location: Lesotho, South Africa, and southern Botswana
Characteristics: Omen of doom, sharp teeth, shapeless, multiple tongues
Lookalike: Yamata-no-Orochi (Japanese)

The Kholomodumo was a shapeless, swallowing monster that got bigger the more it ate. It fed on humans, animals, village huts, and anything else in its path, and symbolized disaster.

I descend on villages like a terrible storm, consuming everyone and everything, and growing impossibly large.

Said to have sharp spikes on its body

Rompo

An African beast, the Rompo had the face of a hare, the legs of a bear, and the elongated claws of a badger. It lured humans and then fed on their flesh.

> I hunt humans at night. They come straight to me when they hear my hypnotic song.

Rompo was said to be covered with coarse hair, like that of a skunk.

Super facts

Pronunciation: ROM-poh
Origin: African mythology   **Location:** Africa and India
Characteristics: Nocturnal hunter, strong, muscular, clawed
Lookalike: Yamata-no-Orochi (Japanese)

The Queen of Sheba

In the religious texts of Jews, Christians, and Muslims, the Queen of Sheba (*SHEE-ba*) was the monarch of an ancient Arabian kingdom. She once led a camel expedition to King Solomon's court in Israel to bring him gifts of gold, jewels, and spices. She then tested his wisdom with a series of riddles.

Mokoi

Super facts

Pronunciation: moh-koy
Meaning: Evil ghost
Origin: First Australian folklore
Location: Australia and Oceania
Characteristics: Spirit, hunter, soul thief
Associations: Death, harm, misfortune

The evil spirit from First Australian folklore, the Mokoi was said to punish sorcerers who used black magic. The Mokoi also sought children to provide it with their life energy.

I am responsible for the deaths of all humans, which I often cause through accident or disease.

Was usually shown as a dark, shadowy figure that lurks in thick forests

Malingee

Malingee was a dangerous spirit from First Australian mythology that used a stone knife or axe to kill anyone that crossed its path. It is often depicted as a tall and thin human-like creature dressed in a loincloth.

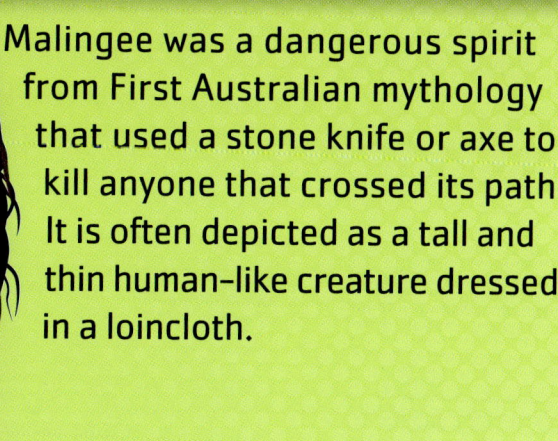

I have smouldering eyes that look like two lumps of burning coal in the dark.

Malingee has two stone knees that make a terrible, scraping sound.

Super facts

Pronunciation: mal-IN-jee **Meaning:** Evil
Origin: First Australian mythology
Location: Central Australia
Characteristics: Glowing eyes, tall, thin, spirit form
Associations: Evil, forests, night

275

Endings

Just as every culture has a story about creation, their myths have also predicted how the world would end. Some said the Earth would be destroyed in a massive natural disaster. Others believed everyone would die in a terrible last battle.

The Sun Stone showing the Aztec calendar

Sun cycle

The Aztecs believed the world went through a series of cycles, each ending in destruction and the creation of a new Sun. According to this theory, the world has been destroyed four times and is today in its fifth Sun.

Ragnarök

In Norse mythology, the Universe would end in a last battle between the gods and giants, called Ragnarök. Although this battle would destroy everything, a few gods would survive to create a new Universe.

The great flood

In some mythologies, gods unleashed a great flood over the Earth to destroy everything. This was sometimes seen as punishment for wrongdoings committed by humans. Often, however, some people survived to start a new age.

Kalki is shown on a white horse with a fiery sword that blazes like a comet.

Kalki

In Hindu mythology, Kalki is the final incarnation of the god Vishnu. It is predicted that Kalki will appear at the end of the current age to destroy the wicked and evil, allowing a new era to begin.

Maitreya

In Buddhism, Maitreya [*may-trey-ya*] is the future Buddha who will descend to Earth at the end of the current age. Maitreya will then begin the teachings of Buddha, which by that time will have been forgotten.

Glossary

abundance
Existing in large amounts

ambush
Act of waiting in a hidden position,
ready to launch a surprise attack

ancestor
Ancient relative

assassinate
Secretly target and murder a particular person

auspicious
Something that brings good luck or positive outcomes

avatar
God appearing on Earth in human or animal form

benevolent
Intending or showing kindness, generosity, and goodwill

bountiful
In large quantities

cannibal
Person who eats the flesh of other humans

chariot
Two-wheeled vehicle pulled by horses

cosmic
Related to the Universe or outer space

creator being
Powerful being who created the Universe
and everything in it

curse
to bring upon great trouble or harm on someone
using supernatural powers

deceased
Dead

deity
God or goddess

depiction
Representation of someone, especially in a work
of art

devour
Eat up something hurriedly, especially when
very hungry

dispute
Disagreement or argument between people

disrupt
To interrupt or disturb, or cause disorder

elements
Parts or components of something, especially in science or nature

embark
To begin a journey, adventure, or important task

eternal
Lasting or existing forever

excavation
To dig into the ground and uncover objects from the past

expedition
Journey with a specific purpose

exploits
Heroic or exciting acts, often showing adventure, courage, or skill

fatal
Causing death

fated
Certain to happen, often beyond one's control

fertility
Ability to create life, from producing offspring to growing crops

fierce
Powerful and wild in a way that is frightening

foresight
Ability to see into or tell the future

forge
Create, shape, or strengthen something

grotesque
Strange, ugly, or distorted in an unnatural way

harpoon
Spear-like weapon attached to a long rope, and used to attack someone

harvest
Refers to the season of gathering crops, or the crops collected in a single growing season

humanoid
Resembling a human in shape, appearance, or behaviour

hymn
Song that is sung in prayer

immortality
Quality of living and lasting forever

inaccessible
Difficult or impossible to reach

indestructible
Something or someone that cannot be destroyed

infallible
Incapable of making mistakes

invader
Person who forcefully enters another's area, often to take control of it

labyrinth
Confusing and complex set of paths, in which it's difficult to find your way through

lair
Place where an animal rests or hides

marine
Related to the sea

mead
Drink made from honey and water

misfortune
Bad luck or a series of unfortunate events

moisture
Tiny amounts of water found in air, soil, or on surfaces

obsidian
Type of volcanic rock that is glassy and very sharp

omen
Something that is seen as a sign of what's to come

paralyse
To cause someone to lose the ability to move or feel sensation in the body

peril
Great danger or risk

plague
Deadly disease that spreads widely

plumage
Feathers covering a bird's body, often colourful

primordial
Existing at or since the beginning of time

prophecy
Prediction or message about what could happen in the future

prosperity
State of success, wealth, or good fortune

quarrel
Heated argument or disagreement between people

realm
Kingdom

rune
Ancient symbol or letter carved onto wood or stone, and believed to hold magic

sacred
Considered holy or deserving great respect

scuttle
Move hurriedly with quick, short steps

seafaring
Related to travelling on the sea

seize
To take hold of something suddenly

slumber
To sleep, especially peacefully

smoulder
Burn slowly without flame, often producing smoke

sorcerer
Person who seeks to control using magical powers

spindle
Long, thin pin or stick by which the thread is twisted in a spinning wheel

stagger
Move unsteadily as if about to fall

sterility
Inability to create life, from producing offspring to growing crops

summon
To issue an order of attendance

tyrannical
Unfair and cruel use of power over other people

unsuspecting
Unaware of danger or harm

venture
To travel somewhere

vindictive
Showing a strong and unreasonable desire to seek revenge

wasteland
Barren land, no longer used for building or growing things

whirlpool
Swirling mass of water that can pull objects down into its centre

wicked
Evil or corrupt

Index

Acknowledgements

DK would like to thank the following people for their assistance in the preparation of this book:

Mitravinda V K and Shipra Jain for design support; Laura Gilbert for proofreading; Helen Peters for the index.

The publisher would like to thank the following for their kind permission to reproduce their photographs:

(Key: a-above; b-below/bottom; c-centre; f-far; l-left; r-right; t-top)

1 Dorling Kindersley: Pham Quang Phuc (cb). 2 Getty Images / iStock: duncan1890 (bl). 3 Adobe Stock: matiasdelcarmine (c). 5 Adobe Stock: Nelson (br). Dreamstime.com: Matias Del Carmine (tr); Anja Koeberle (tc). 10 Dreamstime.com: Vectomart (cl). 11 Dreamstime.com: Rudall30 (cl). 12 Alamy Stock Photo: Chronicle (t); Alida Latham / DanitaDelimont.com (bl). 13 Bridgeman Images: NPL - DeA Picture Library (tl). Getty Images: Werner Forman / Universal Images Group (bl). 14 Adobe Stock: Nelson (cr). Shutterstock.com: John_Mic (c). 15 123RF.com: Tatyana Borozenets (c). 16 Alamy Stock Photo: Encyclopaedia Britannica / Universal Images Group North America LLC (br). 17 Alamy Stock Photo: Azoor Photo (cr); Ivy Close Images (tl). 19 Dreamstime.com: Martin Malchev (tr). 20 Dreamstime.com: Ernest Akayeu (tl, cl). 21 Dreamstime.com: Olga Kurbatova (tr, b). 25 Dreamstime.com: Arkadii Ivanchenko (crb). 26 Dreamstime.com: Matias Del Carmine (tl, cr). 27 Dreamstime.com: Matias Del Carmine (tr, l/Loki). 28 Adobe Stock: Nelson (tl, cr). 29 Adobe Stock: matiasdelcarmine (tr, l). 38 Alamy Stock Photo: The History Collection (bc). 41 Depositphotos Inc: Liliya.Butenko (tr, b). 42 Alamy Stock Photo: jvphoto (c). Dreamstime.com: Vlad Diaconu (bl). 42-43 Adobe Stock: matiasdelcarmine (b). 43 Library of Congress, Washington, D.C.: (tl). 44 Alamy Stock Photo: Pictures From History / CPA Media Pte Ltd (bc). 48 Adobe Stock: Nelson (tl, r). 50 Alamy Stock Photo: Zev Radovan / BibleLandPictures (tl); WHPics (cr). 51 Getty Images: DEA / G. DAGLI ORTI / De Agostini (cr); Leemage / Corbis (bl). Shutterstock.com: Gianni Dagli Orti (tl). 52 Dreamstime.com: Volodymyr Polotovskyi (bl); Deiby Vargas (tl). 52-53 Dreamstime.com: Deiby Vargas. 58 Alamy Stock Photo: Dinodia Photos (bl). Getty Images / iStock: Vera Orlova (tl). 59 Getty Images / iStock: Vera Orlova. 60-61 Dreamstime.com: Vectomart. 63 Alamy Stock Photo: Chronicle (tr). 65 Shutterstock.com: Chintung Lee (tl). 66-67 Shutterstock.com: JianYe Liu. 68 Adobe Stock: Nelson (tl, r). 69 Adobe Stock: Nelson (tr, l). 70 Dreamstime.com: Matias Del Carmine (tl, cr). 71 Adobe Stock: matiasdelcarmine (tr, l). 80 123RF.com: Tatyana Borozenets (tl, r). 81 123RF.com: Tatyana Borozenets (tr, l). 83 123RF.com: Tatyana Borozenets (tr, l). 84-85 Shutterstock.com: klyaksun. 87 Adobe Stock: Nelson (tr, b). 88 Dorling Kindersley: Pham Quang Phuc (tl, c). 90-91 Alamy Stock Photo: CM Dixon / Heritage Images / The Print Collector. 92 Dreamstime.com: Ulf Huebner (br). Shutterstock.com: delcarmat (tl). 93 Shutterstock.com: delcarmat (r). 96-97 Alamy Stock Photo: Granger, NYC. / GRANGER - Historical Picture Archive. 98 Dreamstime.com: Onyxprj (tl). 100 Dreamstime.com: Peter Hermes Furian (tl); Whpics (bl). 101 Dreamstime.com: Peter Hermes Furian. 103 Shutterstock.com: John_Mic (tr, b). 108 Adobe Stock: matiasdelcarmine (tl, r). 111 Alamy Stock Photo: Joerg Reuther / imageBROKER.com GmbH & Co. KG (br). Dreamstime.com: Ben Goode (cl); Ken Griffiths (tl). 116 Alamy Stock Photo: The Print Collector (c). Dreamstime.com: EPhotocorp (tl). 117 Alamy Stock Photo: Darling Archive (t); Ivy Close Images (clb).

Dreamstime.com: Anja Koeberle (br). 118 Dreamstime.com: Matias Del Carmine (c). 118-119 Dorling Kindersley: Pham Quang Phuc (c). 124 Dorling Kindersley: Pham Quang Phuc (cl). Dreamstime.com: Matias Del Carmine (cr). Getty Images / iStock: Vincent_St_Thomas (bl). 125 Alamy Stock Photo: World History Archive (br). 126-127 Dreamstime.com: Meinzahn. 128-129 Dorling Kindersley: Pham Quang Phuc. 128 Dorling Kindersley: Pham Quang Phuc (tl). 130-131 Alamy Stock Photo: Pictures From History / CPA Media Pte Ltd. 133 Shutterstock.com: delcarmat. 134 Alamy Stock Photo: Album (bc). 138 Alamy Stock Photo: Album (clb). Getty Images / iStock: Natalia Barashkova (tl). 138-139 Getty Images / iStock: Natalia Barashkova. 140 Alamy Stock Photo: The Print Collector / Heritage Images (cl). 140-141 Alamy Stock Photo: The Print Collector / Heritage Images (b). 142-143 Alamy Stock Photo: The Protected Art Archive. 144 Shutterstock.com: Eroshka (c). 144-145 Dreamstime.com: Artur Kutskyi. 145 Shutterstock.com: Rohan Vasant Nagwekar (cl). 148 Getty Images: Photostock-Israel / Science Photo Library (crb). 150 Dorling Kindersley: Pham Quang Phuc (tl, b). 152 Dorling Kindersley: Pham Quang Phuc (bl). Dreamstime.com: Artur Kutskyi (cr/Water). Shutterstock.com: Rohan Vasant Nagwekar (cr). 153 Adobe Stock: Anna (tr). Dorling Kindersley: Pham Quang Phuc (cl). 155 Adobe Stock: matiasdelcarmine (tr, b). 156 Dorling Kindersley: Pham Quang Phuc (tl). 156-157 Dorling Kindersley: Pham Quang Phuc. 157 Dorling Kindersley: Pham Quang Phuc (r). 158 Dorling Kindersley: Pham Quang Phuc (tl, bl). 162 Adobe Stock: fergregory (cr). Alamy Stock Photo: Bill Greenblatt / UPI (tl). 163 Alamy Stock Photo: The Picture Art Collection (cla, tr); Impaint (cra); jgaunion / Panther Media GmbH (bl). 168 Shutterstock.com: Eroshka (tl, c). 172-173 Dorling Kindersley: Pham Quang Phuc. 174 Dorling Kindersley: Pham Quang Phuc (cl). Shutterstock.com: Photo craze (cr). 175 Dorling Kindersley: Pham Quang Phuc (cr). Dreamstime.com: The Img (tl). Getty Images / iStock: Nannapat Pagtong (c). 176 Dreamstime.com: Aryo Hadi (tl, c). 178 Alamy Stock Photo: Art Media / Heritage Images / The Print Collector (bl). Dorling Kindersley: Pham Quang Phuc (tl). 179 Dorling Kindersley: Pham Quang Phuc. 180-181 Dorling Kindersley: Pham Quang Phuc. 183 Dreamstime.com: The Img (tr, cl). 186 Dreamstime.com: Ernest Akayeu (tl, r). 188-189 Alamy Stock Photo: The Granger Collection. 190 Getty Images / iStock: duncan1890 (b). 191 Dorling Kindersley: Pham Quang Phuc (cl, b). 192 Alamy Stock Photo: Artotop / Penta Springs Limited (bl). Dorling Kindersley: Pham Quang Phuc (tl). 193 Dorling Kindersley: Pham Quang Phuc (tr, b). 197 Dorling Kindersley: Pham Quang Phuc (b). 198-199 Dorling Kindersley: Pham Quang Phuc (b). Getty Images / iStock: Nannapat Pagtong (t). 200-201 Dorling Kindersley: Pham Quang Phuc. 202 Alamy Stock Photo: Godong / robertharding (cl). Dreamstime.com: Evgeny Fesenko (b). 203 Alamy Stock Photo: Ivy Close Images (tr); Pictures Now (cl). Getty Images / iStock: duncan1890 (br). 207 Shutterstock.com: Photo craze. 208-209 Dorling Kindersley: Pham Quang Phuc. 210 Dorling Kindersley: Pham Quang Phuc. 212 Dreamstime.com: Abhishek4383 (tl). 212-213 Dreamstime.com: Abhishek4383. 213 Alamy Stock Photo: CBW (br). 214-215 Dorling Kindersley: Pham Quang Phuc. 216 Dorling Kindersley: Pham Quang Phuc (bl, cra). 217 Dorling Kindersley: Pham Quang Phuc (b). 219 Dorling Kindersley: Pham Quang Phuc (tr, b). 220-221 Alamy Stock Photo: Alain

Guilleux. 222 Dorling Kindersley: Pham Quang Phuc (bl). 223 Dorling Kindersley: Pham Quang Phuc (b, r). 224 Dreamstime.com: Taily_sindariel (c). 225 Dreamstime.com: Taily_sindariel. 228-229 Dorling Kindersley: Pham Quang Phuc. 230 Dreamstime.com: Leshabu (cr). 231 Adobe Stock: Apolinarias (tl). 232 Dorling Kindersley: Pham Quang Phuc (cr). Dreamstime.com: Vectomart (c). 233 Dreamstime.com: Amy Sachar (cr). Getty Images / iStock: bazzier (c). 234 Alamy Stock Photo: Art Collection 2 (br). 238-239 Adobe Stock: matiasdelcarmine. 240-241 Adobe Stock: matiasdelcarmine. 246 Dreamstime.com: Matias Del Carmine (tl, l). 248 Dreamstime.com: Macrovector (tl, c). 249 Adobe Stock: matiasdelcarmine (tr, c). Dreamstime.com: Macrovector (br). 250-251 Alamy Stock Photo: Keith Corrigan. 252 Alamy Stock Photo: Charles Walker Collection (bl). 255 Getty Images / iStock: bazzier (tr, b). 257 Dreamstime.com: Amy Sachar. 259 Alamy Stock Photo: Xinhua CANADA-MISSISSAUGA-CHINA-BALLET-MULAN ZouxZheng PUBLICATION (crb). 260 Dreamstime.com: Vectomart (tl, c). 261 Dreamstime.com: Arunpv500 (tr, c); Vectomart (br). 262 Alamy Stock Photo: booksR (bl). 264 Dorling Kindersley: Pham Quang Phuc (bl). 265 Dorling Kindersley: Pham Quang Phuc (tr, cl). 267 Shutterstock.com: Hatteviden (tr, b). 268-269 Alamy Stock Photo: Peter Horree. 272-273 Getty Images / iStock: Dorling Kindersley. 276 Alamy Stock Photo: Charles Walker Collection (bl); Classic Image (cr). 277 Alamy Stock Photo: Charles Walker Collection (cl); Ricard Altes Molina (tr). Dreamstime.com: Checco (br). 281 Alamy Stock Photo: Darling Archive (t). 283 Dreamstime.com: Martin Malchev (br). 284 Alamy Stock Photo: Encyclopaedia Britannica / Universal Images Group North America LLC (bl)

Cover images: *Front:* Adobe Stock: Nelson bl; Dorling Kindersley: Pham Quang Phuc cr, cra; Dreamstime.com: Aryo Hadi tr, Vectomart tc; *Back:* Adobe Stock: matiasdelcarmine bc, Nelson bl; Alamy Stock Photo: The Print Collector cra; Dorling Kindersley: Pham Quang Phuc cb, tc; Dreamstime.com: Matias Del Carmine clb, Rudall30 tl, Vectomart cl, crb; *Spine:* Dreamstime.com: Matias Del Carmine t